Dynamic
PROFESSIONAL SELLING

Dynamic
PROFESSIONAL SELLING

Arnold L. Schwartz

Nichols Publishing/New York

Nichols Publishing, P.O. Box 96, New York, NY 10024

Books bearing the Nichols Publishing imprint are published
by GP Publishing, Inc.

Library of Congress Cataloging-in-Publication Data

Schwartz, Arnold L.
  Dynamic Professional Selling

  1. Selling.   I. Title.
HF5438.25.S34   1988   658.8′5   88-19708
ISBN 0-89397-316-5

Dedication

I dedicate this book to all salespeople, the men and women who live with uncertainty, loneliness, rejection, disappointment, turndowns, "maybes," "I'll think it overs," abusive customers, broken appointments, late flights, crowded highways, insensitive sales managers, endless reports, unrealistic corporate planners, product designers who don't understand what the customer needs or wants, stockholders who clamor for more profit in an already saturated marketplace—and who, last but not least, live with their own self-doubts and fears.

Salespeople, the men and women who make the economy go and grow, who convince prospects that there is indeed a better mousetrap (and why not take two)—and who make America and indeed the Western World, the place where dreams really do come true.

To my wife Phyllis, who has steadfastly weathered the highs and lows of my sales career while raising our four daughters and who, with a single finger, laboriously did the typing and stood by me as we nurtured our fragile little enterprise into being.

To Mort Klingon, my first Burroughs sales manager, mentor, adviser, and friend, who served as a role model for what a sales professional and manager of people should act like.

Contents

Introduction

Dynamic Professional Selling is about becoming a sales professional, mastering the art of self-motivation, the motivation of others, and the skills of top-level selling.

This book will show you how to motivate yourself to reach your full potential, raise your self-image, and build self-confidence. You will learn to rise above your self-imposed limitations and become the person you are destined to become. You will see yourself as the winner you are and the even *bigger* winner you can be. You will be able to tap into your reserve of unused talents and abilities and put forth your best efforts at all times.

Dynamic Professional Selling shows you how to develop a better understanding of buyer behavior. You will learn how to build the kind of trust and rapport that puts your message across with greater acceptance and to get on the same wavelength as your prospects.

You will discover proven, exciting techniques for uncovering new business and getting firm appointments with qualified decision makers. You will also learn questioning methods that not only identify needs, but intensify them as well. After reading *Dynamic Professional Selling*, you will be able to make more persuasive group and one-on-one presentations; handle objections more comfortably; and become a strong, effective closer.

You will perform these skills in a professional, relationship-enhancing manner, free from pressure, manipulation, or gimmicks. You will get more accomplished on each sales call, each day, each week, and each month by learning how to set goals and priorities. You will operate in a preactive mode, in charge of your career and your life instead of simply reacting to situations created by others.

The ideas, techniques, and methods presented in *Dynamic Professional Selling* are a result of my thirty-five years of selling experience as sales representative, branch manager, regional manager, national sales manager, sales vice president, business owner, trainer/motivator, and sales consultant.

During my career, I have worked—and trained thousands of sales people—in industries such as office equipment, printing, electronics, banking, insurance, transportation, data communications, financial services, computers, food, publishing, video and audio systems, cosmetics, wines and spirits, ready-to-wear, and real estate.

The salespeople of our client companies (some of which are listed below) have benefited from the ideas you are about to read. You will, too.

Winners believe that, "When you stop getting better, you stop being good."

The goal of this book is to make you even a bigger winner. You're on your way now.

Bon Voyage.

Client List

Some of the companies and organizations who have benefited from Achievement Concept's training program on the "Dynamics of Professional Selling" are:

Agfa-Gevaert
Alexandra de Markoff
Allied Chemical
Almay
American Management
    Association
American Marketing
    Association
AT&T
Avon Books
Bantam Books
Beatrice Foods
Brooks Brothers Clothes
Brunswick Corporation
Burroughs
BVD Company
Camera Mart
Cartier, Inc.
Chroma Copy International
Citibank, N.A.
Citizen Watch Company of
    America
Clairol
Computer Sciences

Cosmair, Inc.
Datatel Minicomputer
    Corporation
Dell Publishing
Digital Communications
    Associates
Dreyfus Ashby and Co., Inc.
Exquisite Forms Industries
First Federal Savings and
    Loan
FTC Communications
Geoffrey Beene
Graphnet
The Guardian Life
    Insurance Co.
Hoffman Video
Ilford, Inc.
International Flavors &
    Fragrances
Jacques Borel Enterprises
Jaz Paris
JVC Company of America
Kobrand Corporation
Konica U.S.A.

KBI, Systems
Longines/Wittnauer
L'oreal/Lancome
McCormack & Dodge
MCI International
Meridian Health Care
Midwest Communications
  Corporation
Mitsubishi Electric Sales
  America, Inc.
Mitsubishi Pro Audio Group
National Association of
  Printers & Lithographers
NEC America
Olympus
Omega Watch Company
Panafax Corporation
Panasonic Broadcast Systems
  Corporation
Penthouse International, Ltd.
Periphonics Corporation
Plessey Communications
  Systems, Ltd.
Quantel
Quick International Courier

RCA Global Communications
Richard D. Irwin, Inc.
Sales & Marketing Execs. of
  Greater N.Y.
Schenley Industries
Sealtest Foods
Seiko Time Corporation
Sharp Electronics
  Corporation
Shortline Tours
Showtime/The Movie
  Channel
Siemens Corporation
Sony National Accounts
Sony Professional Broadcast
Sony Professional Tape
Sony Professional Video
Sterling Drug, Inc.
TNT, Skypak
Trans-Lux Corporation
Treadway Inns
TRT Telecommunications
The *Wall Street Journal*
Universal Microfilm
Warner Computer Systems

1
Overcoming Negativism and Self-defeating Attitudes

I get discouraged, negative, worried, depressed, and fed up. Help!

How can some people be so rude and insensitive? They don't even regard salespeople as part of the human race.

I've heard all about positive thinking, but how do you stay positive with bills to pay, your boss on your back, competitors who discount, and lousy deliveries?

You are a salesperson. But sometimes you wonder, why?

Sure your time is your own, you meet a lot of interesting people, and you know that the potential to earn "big bucks" is there.

And yes, you are aware that to be successful you don't necessarily have to have graduated from an Ivy League school with a 3.9 average and dean's list credentials. Why, your cousin Merwyn, who drives that expensive foreign car, owns an upscale condo, and takes exotic vacations, is a very successful salesperson, and he never impressed you as being too swift in the cerebral department.

It doesn't sound too bad. Especially the "big bucks" part. And, interestingly enough, it is all basically true. You do have considerable independence and freedom of action, you do meet quite a few interesting and even fascinating people, and there is usually an opportunity to earn an income that ranges from above average to extraordinary.

However, there are probably some other aspects of selling that raise your doubts as to whether the selling profession is for you—whether you can achieve the degree of success you want.

Let's face it. Who likes to be disappointed, denied, turned down, ignored, treated with disrespect, belittled, hung up on, criticized, abused, humbled, and out sold by competitors? These are all forms of rejection, and rejection hits us where it hurts the most . . . in our egos, our self-respect, our self-images.

And then there is the uncertainty—the risk. Will I achieve my sales quota? Will that big deal come through? How will external factors such as the economy, government regulations, and new tax laws affect my productivity? Can the factory deliver on time?

In selling, you are exposed to circumstances outside your control on a daily basis. It's part of the job. In selling, you fail more than you succeed. No matter how worthy your product or beneficial your service, there are customers who will buy on price, select another brand, or prefer to do business with someone else.

The single biggest reason that salespeople fail is their inability to deal with rejection. The "nos" wear them down and leave them disillusioned and defeated.

How can we conquer this insidious enemy within and claim the rich rewards that await us? Are you ready for the answer? Here it is.

The PEP Formula—The Winners' Formula for Success

I have developed a simple formula that I use to get me back on the selling track when I am temporarily derailed (which unfortunately still happens). It is called the PEP formula—the winners' formula for success.

PEP is an acronym for persistence, enthusiasm, and planning, the three basic ingredients for successful selling and living. Let's see how we can use this formula to get our attitudes and actions back on the positive side of the ledger.

Persistence

The first ingredient is *persistence*. Nothing in your sales career is more important. The stories of highly successful people who persisted despite overwhelming obstacles and defeat are legion:

Abraham Lincoln, who failed in business, was rejected in marriage, had two unsuccessful bids for Congress, lost three sons before they reached their nineteenth birthdays, and who before being elected president in 1860 was defeated in his bids for the Senate in 1854, the vice presidency in 1856, and the Senate again in 1858.

Chester Carlson, who developed the process in 1938 but had to persevere for twenty-one years before the first Xerox 914 copier came off the assembly line.

Ty Cobb, who was released from his first professional baseball contract after batting only 237 and later became the greatest hitter of all time.

Chuck Yeager, who on his first flight as a passenger threw up all over the back seat and vowed that he would never go back up again and then became the first man to break the sound barrier.

The man who confessed, "Some people think that good salesmen are born not made but I had no natural talent. Most of my colleagues were a lot more relaxed and outgoing than I was. For the first year or two I was stilted and theoretical." That poor soul is Lee Iacocca.

Why is it that when we consider the achievements of successful people, we rationalize that they are different than us—that God gave them special talent—that they have the Midas touch?

Perhaps it is because we only see them in their moments of victory. We don't see them when they are getting up off the deck and back into the fray.

The following three words may just be the most important in this book: *Failure isn't final.* Failure isn't final—unless you permit it.

When you lose a deal, you may have failed to get the order, but you are not a failure. Life is not an undefeated season. To quote Mike Todd, the great promoter, "Being broke is temporary, being poor is a state of mind." Milt Putterman, former president of JAZ Watches, likes to put it this way, "You've got to be able to take a lemon and turn it into lemonade." Out of every adversity a success is born if one looks for it. Find out why you lost the deal and learn from your mistakes. After a while, you will surely turn your defeats into victories.

Remember that nothing worthwhile comes easy. View every experience as a learning experience. View setbacks not as stumbling blocks but rather as building blocks to your ultimate goal of excellence. There is no substitute for hard work and effort. As Woody Allen remarked, "Success is 80 percent showing up and 20 percent luck." "Selling is 95 percent shoe leather," my first zone manager, teacher, and friend, Mort Klingon, used to say at Burroughs.

What is *persistence*? It's doing your paperwork when it's dark (before 9:00 A.M. and after 5:00 P.M.—not during prime selling time). It's making that "extra" call at the end of a weary day, it's pressing for the order one more time, it's asking more questions until you fully understand your prospect's problem, it's studying your product and applications again and again, it's working on that presentation one more time until it rolls off your tongue precisely the way you want it to, it's continuing to do things you know are right despite what others may say, think, or do. These are the actions of the persistent salesperson. Winners put out the effort up front for an unguaranteed result down the line. Losers say, "Pay me now—then I'll do it."

Persistence, a "will-not-be-denied" attitude, is the first, and key, element in the success formula.

A woman approached Fritz Kreisler, the great violinist, after one of his recitals saying, "I would give my life to play as beautifully as you." His response: "Madam, I have!"

Michael Dukakis failed to get his own party's nomination for a second term as governor of Massachusetts. His career seemed shattered.

However, he used the time in private life to reassess his behavior. He recaptured the governorship in the next election and won the democratic presidential nomination in 1988.

He was subsequently defeated by a man who himself failed to win his party's nomination eight years earlier—George Bush.

If there is *one* quality of character that will virtually ensure your success in selling, it is having the courage and self-discipline to persevere in spite of obstacles, setbacks, and rejections.

Enthusiasm

Enthusiasm is the second element in the PEP success formula. If persistence is the fuel, then enthusiasm is the spark that lights the fire. Enthusiasm means enjoying your work, the people you meet, and the world around you. It is not doing what you like, but rather learning to like what you do that will increase your overall enjoyment of your work—and your life.

Charles M. Schwab, who rose from laborer to chairman of Bethlehem Steel expressed it this way: "A man can succeed at anything for which he has enthusiasm."

Selling has its mundane and downright unpleasant aspects. Seemingly endless reports and meetings, the pressure of meeting quotas, cold prospecting, competition, travel, customer complaints, unfathomable company policies, unfeeling bosses, and rejections and disappoint-ments from prospects and customers. These can make selling a chore, and they often do. But don't dwell on these aspects. Instead, focus your energies on the positives such as the independence selling affords, the opportunity to earn an income based on personal production and ability, and the variety of activities that keep you mentally sharp and stimulated.

Recapture the zest you once felt about yourself, your product, and your company. Take your cassette recorder and make a thirty-second "commercial" on *you*. Feature your unique strengths, talents, and abilities (the things that make you special) and listen to it everyday. Become sold on yourself, because once you do, selling your prospects, your boss, your wife, anyone will be easier.

Imagine being hired as an advertising or public relations consultant to promote your product or service. The first thing you would probably do is immerse yourself in the product or service to experience its benefits from the customer's viewpoint. You would get excited about the product so you could promote it enthusiastically.

How does the scenario just described compare to your current attitudes about selling? Are you a little jaded in the way you are presenting your offering? Have you let a few "price" buyers influence your thinking so that you forget that many people buy value not price? Are the cynics in your organization telling you that old-fashioned company loyalty and commitment are out of style?

Remember, you will spend a major part of your life selling your product and your company. Don't give it less than a 100 percent effort. The worst feeling in the world is to look back at something you have tried and wonder how it would have turned out if you gave it your all. Selling is a transference of feeling. It is sharing an honest conviction with another. People buy your belief in what you sell. Enthusiasm is contagious, be a carrier.

I can recall my first job after graduating from Columbia College. Burroughs hired me right off the Morningside Heights campus, and I began working at the Burroughs New York City Branch at Fourth Avenue and Eighteenth Street. We had a roll call each morning in which each salesperson called out the orders he got the preceding day, and the branch manager entered them on a huge blackboard.

Then we all went downstairs to the Southern Coffee Shop for coffee and conversation.

If you sat at the wrong table, you might hear the gloom-and-doomers say, "NCR just released a new accounting machine with a typewriter keyboard. They'll kill us. We can't print names on journals with our Sensimatic. It has no typewriter. They've got more registers (accumulators or memory units), too. We're dead."

After leaving that conversation, all you wanted to do was slit your throat. It didn't make any sense to get out on the street and try to sell.

However, I noticed that several of our salespeople were too "dumb" to know they couldn't bring in business, and they were constantly ringing up the numbers on the board.

The message is clear. The gloom-and-doomers will make sure that their pessimistic predictions come true—for them. So you should hang out with the achievers—the doers. As Henry Ford said, "The person who thinks he can and the person who thinks he can't, are both right." Ralph Waldo Emerson put it this way, "Nothing great was ever achieved without enthusiasm."

Planning

Planning is the PEP success formula's third ingredient. Without planning we tend to drift. We react to situations and events instead of pre-act. Without a master strategy and plan for each account, our sales calls often seem isolated, disconnected, and unrelated. Opportunities are missed because we do not have the overall objective that links seemingly unrelated events. Branch Rickey, president of the old Brooklyn Dodgers expressed this idea well when he said, "Luck is the residue of design" and "Chance favors the prepared individual." "Luck is where planning meets opportunity" was the way Vince Lombardi put it.

Do you have a plan for your territory, your career, your life? Do you have specific goals for the next six months? Year? Five years? Do you have a strategy for each account? Do you plan every sales call, each phone call?

Synergize your persistence and your enthusiasm by channeling them into the areas that will give you the biggest payoff for the time invested. Identify those accounts, those activities, those people that are going to enable you to get the most out of life. Take charge of your life, it's too important to leave to others to control. We don't *plan* to fail, we just *fail* to plan.

I had the experience of working with a large watch company and spending a day in the field with one of its top salespeople, Joe R., to get a flavor of what watch salespeople face on a day-to-day basis. I asked Joe if he had goals for his territory. His reply was that he had set goals, knew virtually every account in his territory, and had identified the ones who had the most potential. Then he added, "Even though they're not all doing business with me now, I know that eventually I'm going to get them and every call I make just takes me one step closer to breaking that account."

Every call Joe made had a purpose—an objective—and he conveyed that attitude to the prospect—you'll be a customer soon.

Joe had a strategy. Do you have a strategy for your territory? Do you know *why* you are calling on certain accounts? Do you have an objective for every sales call, for every phone call? Are you spending your time in a way that will give you the biggest payoff? Or are you gravitating to comfortable low-risk people and activities, even though the possibility of a real return is minimal?

Planning provides a track for you to run on. It gives direction and purpose to your journey. As that famous philosopher, Yogi Berra, once said, "If you don't know where you're going, you may end up somewhere else."

And there you have it—the PEP formula:

Persistence

Enthusiasm

Planning

It is an attitudinal blueprint for your personal success.

And now the best part. You don't have to go back to school, read books, or attend seminars to acquire these ingredients. You already have more than enough persistence, enthusiasm, and planning within your right now to be far more successful than you are.

The stuff that successful salespeople are made of is internal. All you need to do is release it. You are the key factor in your success. If it's going to be, it's up to "thee."

I want to make clear that all the skills and techniques you will find in this book will work only if they are combined with the attitudes described in this first chapter. You see, success is an "inside" job.

You must take personal responsibility for your own motivation and success. Indeed, there is no "free lunch."

The PEP Test

After each sales call, take this quickie test:

1. Was I *persistent* and not deterred by distractions or invalid objections?
2. Was I *enthusiastic* and did I convey my belief in myself, my company, and my product to the buyer?
3. Did I have a *plan* for the call and did I achieve my objective? If not, why?

If you are blaming the product, the territory, the economy, foreign competition, your boss, or others in your organization for your lack of success, you are deluding yourself. These are excuses. Recognize them for what they are. Winners turn these obstacles into opportunities. Losers are defeated by them.

In the words of Theodore Roosevelt, "It is not the critic who counts; not the man who points out how the strong man stumbled, or where the doer of deeds could have done better. The credit belongs to the man who is actually in the arena; whose face is marred by dust and sweat and blood; who strives valiantly; who errs and comes short again and again; who knows the great enthusiasms, the great devotions, and spends himself in a worthy cause; who at the best knows in the end the triumph of high achievement; and who at the worst, if he fails, at least fails while daring greatly, so that his place shall never be with those cold and timid souls who know neither victory or defeat."

This isn't a dress rehearsal. It's your life, your career.

Make it a great one—you can do it!

2
Who Is the You the Buyer Sees?

Sometimes I feel like I'm not as good as the other guys. Do I really belong in those fancy offices with those big shots? They're making three times as much as I am. That's why I take my boss on important deals. I don't want to be embarrassed and humiliated. It's hard to see myself as a real winner.

When I was managing a salesforce selling data services, we wanted our salespeople to sell our automated accounts receivable package as a management information system as opposed to a method of handling "debits and credits." Although our system did the posting, its real benefit was in providing monthly information such as an aged accounts receivable report, sales information, and automatic customer statements.

This approach entailed calling on the owners, presidents, and decision makers of small- to medium-size firms. Often the prospect would try to shunt the salesperson off to the bookkeeper or controller.

Our strong salespeople were able to get to the decision maker and were very successful in bringing in business. Those that called on a lower level were less successful and many of them failed.

What was the difference? Product knowledge, intelligence, education, work ethic—both groups had equal amounts. The critical difference was self-concept, the way the salesperson viewed him or herself.

The successful group felt confident selling to high-level people. They saw themselves as sales consultants helping others run their businesses better. They sold the benefits of more information, delivered faster so that management could make better informed, timely decisions.

The other group was more comfortable calling on lower-level people, people whose success level they perceived to be closer to their own.

They ended up trying to sell a service to buyers who were not interested in the same benefits as their employers and who were more resistant to change.

What enables certain insurance or financial consultants to call on large corporations or on professional people such as physicians and attorneys, sell huge policies or pension plans, and earn high commissions, while their counterparts market to low to moderate earners?

The critical factor is how they see or rate themselves—their self-concept.

Success in selling is more dependent on your attitude than your aptitude, your "want to" as opposed to the "how to." We can learn the "how tos" (product knowledge, presentation skills, features and benefits, handling objections, and closing techniques). But the "want tos" are internal, influenced by years of earlier conditioning and programming. The want tos are the perceptions we have of ourselves, the attitudes that shape our self-concept. Our self-concept is how we see ourselves—our confidence and belief in our ability to cope with life's challenges. It is the value we put on ourselves.

For each of us, what we believe we can accomplish and achieve is limited by our self-concept. In other words:

Low self-concept = low goals
High self-concept = high goals

What is fascinating is that our self-concept often bears no resemblance to our talents and abilities or to how others perceive us. A person with vast talents and abilities who does not acknowledge them or who does not believe he has the ability to achieve his potential is doomed to a life of mediocrity.

Conversely, individuals with only average ability who truly believe they can be top performers are likely to reach or come very close to realizing that belief. Winners expect to win in advance. Life is a self-fulfilling prophecy.

We all have enough potential to be overwhelmingly successful in our sales careers, but we actually use only 20 to 40 percent of our latent talents and abilities. Why? Because our negative attitudes limit our choice of alternatives and prevent us from seeing the vast opportunities that exist for our personal success.

Think about all the "can'ts," "if onlys," and "mind-binders" you've saddled yourself with over the years. Some of my own and others I have heard are:

"I can't stop smoking."

"I'm not a morning person."

"If only I had a better territory."

"I can't lose weight."

"Price is everything."

"It's not what you know, it's who you know."

"I can't save money."

"I can't sell certain personality types."

"If only the commission plan was better."

"I'm not good with figures."

"I can't work with computers."

"If only my boss understood me."

"I'm not handy."

"They don't make'em like they used to."

"I need a vacation."

"I feel lousy."

"I can't make cold calls."

"Why me?"

What are some of your pet "can'ts" and "if onlys?" Write them down so you can examine them and see them for what they really are, self-imposed limitations with little basis in fact. After you have made your list, read them aloud to yourself, but insert the prefix "up to now" before each one.

For example, if one of your *can'ts* is, "I can't seem to get started in the morning," you can get rid of that outdated notion by affirming, "Up to now, I've had trouble getting going in the morning, but from now on . . . ." Stop replaying those old movies of your life in which you played the "heavy" or ended up as the loser. Assign yourself the hero's role in your own life story. You are the author, producer, and director of this saga and can give yourself *any* role you wish.

Thomas Edison refused to accept his teacher's opinion of him as too dumb to stay in school. Albert Einstein flunked math in high school. Franklin Delano Roosevelt wouldn't allow a crippling disease to deter him from his course to greatness.

Creativity

The following is an exercise that illustrates how our thinking is conditioned by past experience. Can you do this exercise in two minutes?

Object: Connect all the dots with four straight lines.

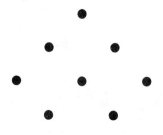

Rules:
1. You cannot retrace (but you can crisscross).
2. You cannot lift the pencil.

Clue: The only thing that will keep you from doing this puzzle in two minutes is a peculiar kind of self-imposed limitation!

Now turn to the end of this chapter to see how this problem is solved.

What this exercise illustrates is that we attempt to solve new problems using old methods. We limit ourselves by the way things were done in the past. To solve this problem, you have to go outside the dots. In other words, you must try alternative approaches, be creative and untethered by past thinking, and seek new ways of doing things. Robin Mumford, then a young director of one of Allied Chemical's fibres divisions, had a pet saying, "Happiness is having alternatives." As professional salespeople, we have to go outside our predetermined, programmed thinking to achieve excellence.

Could the same problem of the dots be solved with only one straight line, without moving the paper or the dots? Let your mind expand, roam, explore, soar. Think before going on. The answer: a wide line made by a thick crayon, paint brush, or roller would do it. Who said the line had to be thin?

How are you handling your accounts, your territory? Are you using the same methods you used three years ago, five years ago, ten years ago? Are you satisfied with the results? Are you working and thinking the way you are because it is the most effective way or is it because it has become comfortable and familiar? Habits take us back to where we were yesterday. If yesterday's results are not totally acceptable, consider a change in your habits. Move outside the dots.

To get started, take a different route coming home from work tonight, get up at a different time, pick up a different newspaper, call a prospect and ask for the president, ask for the order upfront. Do something different, right away.

Attitude Motivation

Attitude motivation is self-motivation. It is internally generated, and it is the most powerful motivation that exists because it means that you're doing whatever you're doing because you see the "what's in it for me" (WIIFM). Contests, prizes, commissions, and recognition quota clubs are fine and they serve to support attitude motivation, but they are external and are controlled by others. You must take personal responsibility for your own motivation.

Attitudes are habits, habits of thought. Courage, courtesy, friend-liness, commitment, and self-control are all attitudes. They are mental habits. They can be developed or changed. An attitude is an enduring inclination to react in the same way each time you find yourself in a similar situation. How do you react when a prospect raises an objection or expresses doubts about your recommendations? What do you do when your closing question is met with "no!" You tend to react similarly in each situation. Is it an appropriate behavior? One you would choose if you made a conscious choice as opposed to an instinctive, automatic response?

Successful salespeople who have developed positive attitudes, realize that their attitudes, or the way they think, will either get them to where they want to go, or will limit them. What are your attitudes? Complete the following checklist and rate yourself. Be honest. It's for your eyes only. The results will give you an indication of what attitudes you need to work on.

Self-Description Questionnaire

Instructions: For each statement, blacken the box that best represents you.

	Very Poor Description	Excellent Description
	1 2 3 4 5	6 7 8 9 10
1. I have a high degree of self-confidence.	☐ ☐ ☐ ☐ ☐	☐ ☐ ☐ ☐ ☐
2. I tend to view every problem situation as an opportunity for growth rather than as a possible pitfall to be avoided.	☐ ☐ ☐ ☐ ☐	☐ ☐ ☐ ☐ ☐
3. I start each day with optimism.	☐ ☐ ☐ ☐ ☐	☐ ☐ ☐ ☐ ☐

4. I am highly creative in finding solutions to problems.   ☐ ☐ ☐ ☐ ☐ ☐ ☐ ☐ ☐ ☐

5. I am a person who takes action rather than one who procrastinates.   ☐ ☐ ☐ ☐ ☐ ☐ ☐ ☐ ☐ ☐

6. I usually complete whatever I begin.   ☐ ☐ ☐ ☐ ☐ ☐ ☐ ☐ ☐ ☐

7. Because I profit from mistakes, I have little fear of failure.   ☐ ☐ ☐ ☐ ☐ ☐ ☐ ☐ ☐ ☐

8. I see myself as a decisive individual.   ☐ ☐ ☐ ☐ ☐ ☐ ☐ ☐ ☐ ☐

9. I have a vast reservoir of undeveloped ability to draw on.   ☐ ☐ ☐ ☐ ☐ ☐ ☐ ☐ ☐ ☐

10. I am a person who creates opportunities rather than one who waits for them.   ☐ ☐ ☐ ☐ ☐ ☐ ☐ ☐ ☐ ☐

11. I have a very favorable self-concept.   ☐ ☐ ☐ ☐ ☐ ☐ ☐ ☐ ☐ ☐

12. I am basically a self-starter.   ☐ ☐ ☐ ☐ ☐ ☐ ☐ ☐ ☐ ☐

13. I believe most people are willing to be helpful if they are asked.   ☐ ☐ ☐ ☐ ☐ ☐ ☐ ☐ ☐ ☐

14. I have the motivation and ability not to be limited by my past.   ☐ ☐ ☐ ☐ ☐ ☐ ☐ ☐ ☐ ☐

15. I expect to become highly successful in my work.   ☐ ☐ ☐ ☐ ☐ ☐ ☐ ☐ ☐ ☐

16. I am highly motivated to strive for excellence in whatever I do.   ☐ ☐ ☐ ☐ ☐ ☐ ☐ ☐ ☐ ☐

17. I have very little tendency toward self-doubt and worry.   ☐ ☐ ☐ ☐ ☐ ☐ ☐ ☐ ☐ ☐

18. I have a clear concept of what I want from life and work.   ☐ ☐ ☐ ☐ ☐ ☐ ☐ ☐ ☐ ☐

19. When I decide what I want, I usually get it.   ☐ ☐ ☐ ☐ ☐ ☐ ☐ ☐ ☐ ☐

20. I live with a strong sense of purpose and direction.   ☐ ☐ ☐ ☐ ☐ ☐ ☐ ☐ ☐ ☐

Place an asterisk by the items where you rated yourself with a "5" or less. What can you do—what will you do—to improve in those areas?

William James, the noted psychologist and father of practical psychology, observed that one of the most marvelous discoveries of his generation "is that man can alter his life by altering his attitude of thought." This means that you can control your own destiny. You can override the old programs, the outdated injunctions, the can'ts and if onlys that limit your achievement and rob you of your potential.

Our attitudes determine our self-concept. Our self-concept is a result of the way we see ourselves, the way we rate ourselves in different aspects of our lives. Let's examine seven key areas of living in which we evaluate ourselves.

1. *Social.* Social development deals in intangibles. Is your personality as you like it? How do you relate to friends and acquaintances? Will you mix at a gathering without discomfort? What do people think of you? Do you have a active social life outside of business?
2. *Mental.* Do you challenge your intellect, read good books, and engage in activities that stimulate your brain and require deductive reasoning and problem solving?
3. *Physical.* How do you look and feel? Do you have a good energy level, stamina? Do you smoke or drink too much, get proper exercise, maintain a healthy weight? How is your blood pressure, cholesterol level, heart?
4. *Financial.* Are your financial obligations under control? Do you meet your commitments or indebtedness promptly? Do you have a systematic plan for building your personal net worth? Do you understand and take advantage of the legal avenues for conserving capital?
5. *Family.* Do you contribute to your family or only take from it? What kind of brother, sister, son, daughter, father, or mother are you? Is your family a source of strength for you?
6. *Career.* Do your job requirements match your aptitudes? Do you enjoy your work? Do you have a future, and if so, are you planning for it? Do you need additional education or training? Do you have a plan for your career development?
7. *Religious/Ethical.* Do you profess one code of moral conduct and behave differently? What do you really believe in—what would you staunchly defend? What are your values and do you live by them? What do you want to be respected and admired for?

The following bar graph illustrates how individuals might rate themselves in each area.

Total Self-Concept

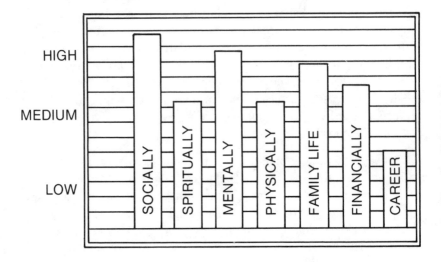

These components of the self-image can be expressed as spokes of a wheel: the Wheel of Life.

Wheel of Life

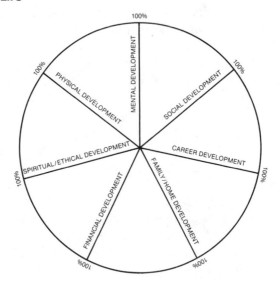

Put a dot on each spoke where you rate yourself at this moment in each of the seven key areas of your life. Now join all the dots, drawing your own personal wheel of life.

How would you like to push that wheel around for the rest of your life? A bumpy ride perhaps. But this is the wheel you are riding on your trip through life. The space between your wheel and the outside wheel represents potential, growth, opportunity. And as we push our wheel out by consciously working on the areas of our lives that are important, the outside wheel moves outward as well, presenting more opportunities for individual growth and achievement in the exciting challenge of life.

The way you have rated yourself is the way you see yourself today—your self-concept. But your self-concept is not static. To push your inner wheel out and become a bigger, more well-rounded person, you need to set goals in the areas of your life that are most important to you.

Write the number "one" next to the spoke representing the area of life most important to you at this time. Then place a two next to the second most important area and so forth. You have now set priorities or values that you can use in goal setting and in helping you clarify what is actually important to you.

Select the spoke or area of your life that you would most like to improve in the next thirty days. Now think of one goal you can achieve that will push your wheel out in that area. Make it specific and measurable with a thirty-day time frame and put a little stretch in it. You have now taken a positive action step in building your self-concept.

For each of us, the "area of the possible," what we believe we are capable of achieving and becoming, is limited by our self-concept.

To expand this area and realize your full potential as an achieving, growing individual, you must see yourself not as you are but as you can be. And you can be whatever you want to be. The good life need not be limited to a fortunate few. You are entitled to all the success you earn by your own effort.

In selling, our self-concept is constantly tested. It is under attack every day, on every sales call. To combat these forays against your self-esteem, use affirmations, self-talk, auto suggestion, and personal "commercials" to reinforce the main theme, which is that you are indeed *lovable* and *capable.*

The first sale in the selling process is the sale you make to yourself. It's selling you, on you.

Success

"Success is the progressive realization of worthwhile, predetermined, personal goals," says Paul Meyer, president of Success Motivation International (SMI). The word progressive indicates that success is ongoing, continuous, a process. You set a goal, move toward it, achieve it and then set another one, hopefully more challenging than the first.

When is it most important to feel successful about your goal?

At the beginning, of course. When you set a goal that is personally meaningful to you and then develop a plan to achieve it, you visualize the achievement throughout the whole process and enjoy the thrill of the chase.

Picture this scene. Tonight in your sleep, a vision appears. The vision proclaims that you have been selected as the "salesperson of the year" in your industry. You are guaranteed success by the forces most high. However, there is one proviso.

You have to continue to work hard or this wonderful gift will be taken from you. Got the picture?

Question: What will you do differently now that you know you cannot fail, that your success is preordained?

Would you call on accounts you are reluctant to call on now, sell to higher levels of authority, dress better, buy a new attache case or even a new car? Would you be happier, less stressed, less anxious, more confident knowing that you are the best there is? What will your life be like? What will change about your attitude, your behavior, your relationships, your approach to your job?

Your overall feeling is positive, isn't it? You feel secure in the knowledge that success is yours.

Then my question to you is, why aren't you doing these things now? Why do you need a fairy-tale story about a vision in the night to do the things you should be doing anyway?

If you seek a virtue, act "as if." Start behaving today as if you are the top performer in the industry. Form a mental picture of the type of person you would ideally like to be, the type of salesperson you want to become, and start acting, thinking, dressing, talking, feeling like that person. Make believe it's a role you are playing in a show— the role of the most successful person you know.

Success is an attitude. It is a planned activity. Believe in yourself. You already possess all the ingredients you need for success.

Go outside the dots. See the many alternatives for your success by being open to constructive change. See yourself not only as you are, but also as you can be. Increase the area of the possible for yourself by taking on new challenges, activities, and relationships. If you stumble a bit in your exploration into areas of uncertainty, remember, "Failure isn't final."

Alternatives!

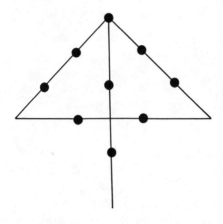

3
Prospecting—The Salesperson's Bane of Existence

Prospecting is pure drudgery. Sometimes I'm actually sorry when I have a good month because I've sold most of my prospects and have to start the dreadful process all over again.

Why don't they call me? You know, I could really enjoy selling a lot more if I didn't have to wade through all those 'not interesteds' and 'call me in six months.'

What's the answer?

Definition of prospecting: identifying, contacting, and attempting to sell to new accounts or new departments in existing accounts or to sell new products and services to present customers. Key word: new.

Selling would be all fun and games if we could wake up each morning knowing that we had a day full of qualified appointments set up for us with interested prospects who were eagerly awaiting our arrival. If this were true, we would probably have a glut in the sales field because in reality, prospecting usually results in a high rejection rate and drives a lot of people out of selling.

No matter how good your product or service is, you need someone to listen to your story. Advertising and direct mail have limitations in getting people to respond, and even those that do respond need to be qualified.

Prospecting is the lifeblood of a business because it brings in new accounts and compensates for the normal attrition every business experiences. The president of a large paper wholesale company estimates that approximately 20 percent of his customers turn over annually. That 20 percent might put the company out of business if they were not replaced by new customers.

Why Do Salespeople Abhor Prospecting?

The answer is obvious. You are setting yourself up for rejection. Often the prospects have never heard of you or your firm, the timing is wrong, they are not in a receptive mood, or they have been bombarded by phone calls. Secretaries screen their bosses' calls and are often curt and impolite. Prospecting can be an unsettling experience.

How do we overcome these negatives and make prospecting a satisfying and productive experience?

To start with, you must develop a prospecting mentality, that is, the acceptance of prospecting as a necessary part of selling; as basic as being well groomed or having product knowledge. Successful salespeople develop a "selective perception" about prospecting. This means they "see the world" in terms of prospective customers for what they are selling. They see prospects everywhere, in restaurants, planes, social situations, and family gatherings. While I am not advocating that you should be talking and thinking business all the time, the dedicated and enthusiastic salesperson is constantly aware of peoples' needs and wants as they relate to what he sells.

Perhaps you are thinking, "That all sounds fine, but I don't like cold calling. Talking to strangers is not my forte. The company should provide leads. They should do more advertising. My time should be spent in selling, not talking to a lot of deadbeats." (The "shoulds" here are really "if onlys.")

You may not appreciate the following response, but this is the way it is.

You don't have to like prospecting—you just have to do it! There are many people out there that need what you are selling but do not respond to advertising, direct mail, or computerized telemarketing. They may, however, respond to a warm, enthusiastic, knowledgeable person who can help them make a decision that is good for them. *Prospecting is often a case of finding the person that is looking for you.* When you find each other, it's love at first presentation. However, in the process, you have to wade through a lot of disinterested suspects and a lot of negative reaction. If you are fortunate enough to have leads provided for you, you still need to qualify them. Even if you have others making appointments for you, my strong recommendation is that you also do some prospecting on your own.

There is an additional benefit to prospecting. When you prospect up a deal, you can skew it to your strengths, build a strong relationship with the buyers, and "spec" the deal to effectively stymie competition. You earn higher margins.

Conversely, when prospects call you, generally they have also called your competitors. You then find yourself in a price war where the only winner is often the customer.

Prospecting tests a salesperson's ego, discipline, and motivation. It is far easier to make presentations to existing customers who you know will accept you or to prospects who have already declared their interest. But whether you are new in the territory or have a solid following, you must develop new business. Prospecting will hone your selling skills, keep you on top of what's happening in the marketplace, and put money in the bank. And surprisingly, you will get good at it and even learn to enjoy the challenge.

Developing a Prospecting System

Prospecting is not a hit-or-miss activity, something you do when you have some time. It is a planned activity that must be scheduled into your selling day or week.

Like depositing part of your paycheck in the bank, if you wait for what's left after meeting all your expenses, your bank account is likely to be "zero." But if you take it off the top and deposit it immediately, you will probably find a way to manage with what's left and have a growing savings account as well.

Prospecting is like that. Do it first and you will never want for a pipeline of prospects and business.

The Steps in the Prospecting System

Step 1: Acknowledge prospecting as the first step in the selling process and the key to your selling success.

"I'd rather be a master prospector than a wizard of speech with no one to tell my story to." Live by this sound advice offered by Paul Meyer, president of SMI.

Selling is a numbers game. The more calls you make, the more appointments you will get; the more appointments, the more presentations; the more presentations, the more sales; the more sales, the more income, recognition, title, and prestige. It all begins with prospecting.

Focus on the end result—not the process. If your average is one appointment for every ten calls, view the nine misses as stepping stones to the one hit! Visualize your new condo, that spiffy sports car, the latest digital audio ensemble in your den, not the fact that nine people missed the opportunity of talking to you.

No one cares how many you lose. It's the ones you win that count. If it takes you more calls to get an appointment than someone else, then make more calls. There are few "natural" salespeople. Most of us have to use our persistence and determination to earn our keep.

Listed below are some of the all-time strikeout leaders in professional baseball. Do you recognize any of these "failures"?

1. Reggie Jackson
2. Willie Stargell
6. Mickey Mantle*
13. Frank Robinson
14. Willie Mays*
22. Hank Aaron*
24. Babe Ruth*

In 50th place on this dubious list is the woeful loser, Pete Rose. (The asterisk indicates a Baseball Hall of Fame member.)

The message is clear: You need to lose some to win some.

Step 2: Establish a prospect profile and classify prospects.

Who should you call on, in what sequence, and in what order? Pareto's principle (the well-known 80/20 rule that states that 20 percent of effort yields 80 percent of the results) suggests that 80 percent of the business comes from 20 percent of the prospects. Lets start by asking who are your best present customers, the ones that give you the biggest payoff for your time invested? What particular need are you satisfying? Do they have a unique problem that your product or service solves better than competition?

What characteristics do they have in common? If you are selling to only one or two vertical markets (lines of business), identifying prospects is relatively easy. But even in this case, it is important to focus on the high-potential users.

When your product has a broad market potential, you have to zero in on a few specific markets and specialize. Salespeople who sell pension plans can sell everyone, but the successful ones select a market such as doctors or CPAs and work that market. They become familiar with the jargon, problems, and proven solutions unique to that line of business. They become experts rather than generalists.

Too many potential prospects can lead to no prospects. You find yourself wandering all over the place with no real plan of action. Decide on the industry classifications you want to penetrate and concentrate in those areas.

Here are some criteria you can use to categorize your best customers:

1. Line of business — SIC code
2. Revenues (i.e., more than $10,000,000 or less than $5,000,000)
3. Number of locations, plants, branches
4. Number of employees
5. Type of distribution (i.e., sells through dealers, direct to end user, etc.)
6. Geographic location
7. International business
8. Net worth, credit rating, etc.
9. Life of present equipment or contracts
10. Obsolescence factors
11. Company's policy and culture affecting purchasing
12. Past experience with your company or product

Creating an Ideal Prospect Profile

Narrow the key factors that describe your "ideal" prospect to a manageable number such as five. Then list them in declining order of importance. In addition to quantitative criteria, you may want to include cultural characteristics such as the company's traditions, values, attitudes, or philosophy. Your ideal prospect company might have a strong "people" orientation or pride themselves on their reputation for creativity and innovation.

You now have a model that you can use to evaluate potential prospects. Figure 3-1 is a sample ideal client profile that will help you analyze your present customers.

Figure 3-1
Ideal Client Profile

Name of client _____

Type of business _____

_____

SIC codes _____

No. of employees _____   Sale volume _____

Divisions or subsidiaries _____

Other information _____

Decision makers _____

_____

Associations client belongs to _____

_____

_____

Client special characteristics as they relate to my business _____

_____

Special needs my product/service fills for client _____

_____

Client's competitors _____

_____

_____

Names of other companies, people, or organizations that have similar
needs _____

_____

_____

Classify your current prospects as to how they fit your ideal profile. Those that have the best fit are "A" prospects. "B" prospects are those that meet most or all of the criteria but to a lesser degree. "C" prospects may meet only one or two of the criteria.

Invest most of your selling efforts in your "A" prospects and customers.

Establishing Call Frequencies

A call frequency schedule will help you to establish guidelines for how to best allocate your time. It ensures that you spend most of your time on high-payoff accounts. Figure 3-2 is a sample call frequency schedule.

Figure 3-2
Call Frequency Schedule

Class	Potential Annual Sales Volume of Accounts	Sales Calls
A	More than $350,000	Once a month
B	$200,000 to $350,000	Once every 2 months
C	$50,000 to $200,000	Once every 4 months
D	Less than $50,000	Once every 8 months (or telephone only)

Call frequency schedules are only guidelines and each account must be looked at individually. Note that prospective customers as well as present accounts are classified by their potential volume. This means that you may be better served to spend more time on an "A" prospect than on a "C" customer. Looking at your territory objectively will prevent you from spending time on unproductive prospects even though they are friendly and easy to see.

I have a "hit list" of key clients who I want to be in constant contact with. The list is with me at all times and serves as a reminder of where I need to focus my efforts. I review this list constantly and add and delete names when necessary. Develop your own "hit list," the 20 percent of your prospects and customers who can produce 80 percent of your business.

Step 3: Find prospects that fit the profile.
A. Existing Customers
One of the best sources of new business are your existing customers. Many salespeople take for granted that their customers know them, remember them, and will call when they have a need. Not so! It is best to assume that "out of sight is out of mind," and make sure that you constantly update your customers on your latest product enhancements, literature, and services. See that they get periodic mailings. Invitations to seminars show them that you are "wooing" their business just as diligently as when you were trying to convert them from prospects to customers. Taking existing clients for granted is what permits competition to invade your accounts. Many a smug salesperson sitting on his laurels has been surprised to learn that the account he thought he had "locked up" was "stolen" by a persistent, hungry competitor who let the customer know he wanted his business and was willing to work for it. Remember, your customer is someone else's prospect.

An international franchiser of professional color labs instituted a telemarketing campaign to contact every customer who had not sent in work for sixty days. They not only found some customer dissatisfaction, most of which they were able to handle, but more importantly uncovered some great potential business. This practice of monitoring existing customers by phone has been extremely successful. In addition, they call each customer after every job to make sure the customer is satisfied, a practice most customers find almost unbelievable. Wouldn't you?
B. Former Customers
Another source of prospects is people that used to buy from you but stopped. Perhaps the reason is no longer valid. Maybe there is a new decision maker who would be open to your suggestions. Examine old records. Look through past invoices to get the names of those accounts and contact them. You may find that the perceived barriers are nonexistent.
C. Directories
A good business library has many kinds of directories. Some of the well-known ones are:
□ *Standard & Poor's*
□ *Million Dollar Directory* (published by Dun's Marketing Services)

☐ Coles publications (street or "reverse" directories)
☐ *Thomas Register*
☐ *Polk's City Directories*
☐ *Gale's Encyclopedia of Associations* and *Directory of Directories*
D. Newspapers and Magazines
These sources provide current information on executive promotions, transfers, and company activities. The classified section indicates which companies are hiring and possibly expanding.
E. Yellow Pages
The yellow pages of your phone book are very good prospecting tools because the listings are by line of business and the addresses and phone numbers are up to date.
F. Seminars
Conducting seminars and open houses and exhibiting at trade shows are excellent ways to find prospects. You multiply your time by attracting many potential prospects to a single location.
G. · Networking
Networking is a burgeoning method for making new contacts in a quasi-social environment that is designed to enable people to increase their spheres of influence. Networking groups are springing up in all areas of the country. Look for ads in local newspapers and talk to other salespeople to get information.
H. Direct Mail/Advertising
Send personal letters to prospects and follow them up with phone calls. Follow up company mailings with phone calls. Advertise in appropriate publications in your territory or area of operation.
I. Public Relations
Write articles, give talks, do community work where you and your company will be recognized.
J. Associations
Joining the associations where your prospects are members will enable you to meet them in a different environment and get to know them on another level. This is a form of networking.
  Making presentations at association meetings is an excellent way to attract prospects. Seek out opportunities to give presentations on how your industry, company, or product impacts the audience's concerns. Keep it non-sales oriented.
K. Cold Calls
This means physically calling on a company or individual without an appointment. Make cold calls when you are already in an area and have limited free time before your next appointment. The chief value of this method is information gathering.

L. Referrals

Referrals are the best, yet underused, method of prospecting. You are missing out if you don't capitalize on the good work you've done for satisfied customers by getting referrals to others that would also like to receive similar benefits. What better way to meet a new prospect than through a recommendation from someone he trusts? You wouldn't hesitate to recommend a good restaurant or movie to a friend. Why should a pleased client hesitate to recommend a good vendor to someone who can use one?

Write down the names of ten of your best clients right now and set a goal to get three referrals from each.

Did you do it?

Here is a referral presentation you might use:

Salesperson: "Bill, I've got a problem and I need your help."

Bill: "Sure, John, how can I help?"

Salesperson: "I need to get the names of five people like yourself. People who are open-minded and receptive to new ideas and who can benefit from my product/service in the same way you have. Who can you suggest, Bill?"

Bill: "Why don't your try Dick Ball over at Hi Tech, Ltd. Tell him I referred you."

Why ask for five referrals? If you ask for one, you might get none. If you ask for five, you are likely to get at least one or two. It's embarrassing to go "0 for 5."

Referrals need not be limited to existing clients. It is a good idea to ask everyone you talk to for referrals. The worst thing that can happen is that you get a "no," so what have you lost?

Sources of prospects are limited only by your creativity and effort. They're out there, and they need what you've got. Develop a prospecting awareness and determination to find them.

You Never Know Where You'll Find Prospects!

A young saleswoman in financial planning stopped off at her parents' home on the way from work. As she crossed through the living room, she spotted a painter, perched on a ladder, busily at work on the ceiling.

Being gregarious by nature, she stopped to chat and introduce herself. After a few moments conversation, the painter asked, "What do you do for a living?" She replied that she was a financial planner and helped people invest their money wisely.

"That's interesting," he said, "I recently received a small inheritance and was wondering what to do with it."

When she told me this story, we were dining at an oceanfront restaurant in a beautiful resort in Cancun, Mexico, where I was addressing the sales leaders of her company. Although she had only recently joined the firm, that sale to the painter helped her to qualify for the trip.

Many salespeople think that their success has a lot to do with luck, just being in front of a prospect at the right time. They don't realize that if they weren't there, talking about their businesses, they would never get lucky. Like the lottery, "you have to be in it to win it."

Step 4: Set up a recordkeeping and follow-up system.
First, remember the KISS rule: Keep it short and simple. The following system is designed as a prospecting system and requires the following materials:

> 3 in. x 5 in. cards in varying colors
> 3 in. x 5 in. card file box
> January to December dividers
> 1 to 31 dividers (these go behind current month)
> A to Z dividers (these go in back or in separate box)
> Business card file (to keep customer business cards in alphabetical order)

Transfer your prospect information to the 3 in. x 5 in. cards. If you have a large territory, use a different color for each geographic area so they are easily identifiable.

The information on the front of the card should include:

> Classification "A," "B," or "C"
> Company name, Address, and Zip code
> Telephone number
> Person(s) to contact (and title)
> Secretary's name
> Any other personal information

The back of the card is used to record the date and result of your last call as well as the scheduled follow-up date.

First, arrange the cards in stacks by geographic area. You may want to use different colors for each geographic area. Then, using any information you have, classify each card as an A, B, or C (A being the best prospect).

Now put the stacks in the sequence you will be calling. Each stack represents a geographic area of your territory and is arranged in an A, B, C order.

Place the stacks that will not be contacted immediately in their appropriate places in the card file, that is, behind the divider of the month you will contact them. You are left with a stack of prospect cards that you will begin contacting immediately.

As you make each call, note the result and the date of the next contact on the back of the card. Place the card behind the appropriate month or day (if in current month) in the file.

You simply keep moving the cards in the file as you make appointments or schedule the next calls. Make sure to jot down pertinent information so you can use it to build trust and rapport on your next contact.

Note: If you've been thinking about starting a prospecting system, here's an action plan:
1. Pick up five hundred 3 in. x 5 in. cards at the stationer today along with the file, dividers, etc.
2. Select the source of your prospects (directories, lists, inactive account files, and so forth).
3. Write out a minimum of fifty prospect cards today.
4. Have two hundred fifty cards prepared by the end of the week.

When you've completed these steps, you're serious about prospecting. You're on your way.

Step 5: Set prospecting goals.
How much time should you devote to prospecting? When is the best time to prospect? How do you set up a prospecting schedule?

It all begins with a goal. The ultimate goal is the amount of sales revenue you want to generate or the number of units or new accounts you want to sell through your prospecting efforts. Let's take a hypothetical case.

Bill Barnes sells widgets. His widgets range in price from $3,000.00 to $10,000.00, and his commission ranges from 7½ percent to 12½ percent depending on the model. His annual salary is $20,000.00, and he is paid commissions in addition to his salary.

Bill Barnes's earnings goal for the year is $50,000.00. Thirty thousand dollars will be in commissions. At an average commission rate of 10 percent, Bill will have to sell $300,000.00 worth of widgets.

The average sale is $5,000.00 so Bill will need to make sixty sales to reach his goal. This means he will need to produce $25,000 in monthly revenues (or five sales per month).

Figure 3-3
Bill Barnes's Prospecting Plan

Salary: $ 20,000.00
Commission goals: $ 30,000.00
Total revenue required to reach goal: $300,000.00
Average sale amount: $ 5,000.00
Commission rate: 10%

Prospecting Productivity Planner

1. My earnings goal for the year/period is $50,000.
2. I need to generate $300,000 in sales for the year/period; $25,000 each month.
3. I need to make 5 (number of) sales to achieve $25,000 in sales each month.
4. I need to make 40 presentations to get 5 sales (1:8).
5. I need to make 160 phone contacts* to get 40 presentations (1:4).
6. I need to make 480 dials to get 160 phone contacts (1:3).

*Contact = reaching the desired individual on the phone.

I will achieve the following productivity goals each week. Making 120 dials, I will:

1. Reach 40 people (contacts) [one contact every three dials].
2. Get 10 appointments (presentations) [one appointment every four contacts].
   Resulting in 1.25 sales [one sale every eight appointments].
   Generating $6,000 in weekly revenue [$5,000 revenue per sale].
   Earning me $600 in weekly commissions [10 percent commission per sale].
3. Designate the following days and hours for phone prospecting each week (based on thirty dials per hour):

Monday and Friday	9:00 A.M. to 11:00 A.M. (4 hours)
Day(s)	Hours

Telephone Batting Average

Dials					Contacts				
1	2	3	4	5	1	2	3	4	5
6	7	8	9	10	6	7	8	9	10
11	12	13	14	15	11	12	13	14	15
16	17	18	19	20					
21	22	23	24	25					
26	27	28	29	30	Appointments				
31	32	33	34	35					
36	37	38	39	40	1	2	3	4	5
41	42	43	44	45	6	7	8	9	10
46	47	48	49	50					

Bill estimates that he needs to have eight prospects to close one sale. This means that he will need to call on forty new prospects a month (five sales x eight prospects) or approximately two per day.

Bill's previous experience with getting appointments indicates that he usually closes one of four phone contacts for an appointment. A phone contact is defined as talking to a qualified decision maker or influencer. He will need to make 160 phone contacts per month to get his forty appointments. (forty appointments x four contacts)

Because not everyone that Bill calls is in, he averages three attempts to make one contact. Therefore, it requires 480 attempted calls (or "dials") to make 160 contacts. The monthly totals look like this:

Dials:	480
Contacts:	160
Appointments:	40
Sales:	5
Revenues:	$25,000.00
Commissions:	$2,500.00

Based on these numbers, Bill earns approximately $5.21 in commissions each time he dials a phone number ($2,500.00 divided by 480).

Based on thirty dials per hour, it will require approximately sixteen hours per month or four hours per week of prospecting time for Bill to reach his goal. Figure 3-3 contains an illustration of Bill's plan.

Step 6: Set up a prospecting schedule.
When is the best time to prospect? It depends on a number of factors: when your prospects are generally in, when you are in your office, and when you are at your telephone best.

The important thing is to schedule the same time each week and be thoroughly prepared with your cards, script, records, and anything else you need to work on the phone.

Have a goal for each session and do not stop calling until you have reached your goal. Then, reward yourself in some way.

To relate what you have just read to your own situation, complete the information in Figure 3-4.

You now have your productivity goals for prospecting. Keep a record of each prospecting session to fine tune the numbers. If it takes you fewer calls to get the desired number of appointments, you can either spend less time on the phone or spend the same amount and make more appointments.

Once you have determined the "inputs" required to achieve your goals, that is, the dials, contacts, and appointments, concentrate on performing those activities.

Figure 3-4
Sample Prospecting Plan

Prospecting Productivity Planner
1. My earnings goal for the year/period is $ _____ .
2. I need to generate $ _____ in sales for the year/period;
   $ _____ each month.
3. I need to make _____ (number of) sales to achieve
   $ _____ in sales each month.
4. I need to make _____ presentations to get _____ sales.
5. I need to make _____ phone contacts* to
   get _____ presentations.
6. I need to make _____ dials to get _____ phone contacts.
*Contact = reaching the desired individual on the phone.

I will achieve the following productivity goals each week. Making-
_____ dials, I will:
1. Reach _____ people (contacts).
2. Get _____ appointments (presentations).
   Resulting in _____ sales.
   Generating $ _____ in weekly revenue.
   Earning me $ _____ in weekly commissions.
3. Designate the following days and hours for phone prospecting
   each week (based on thirty dials per hour):

Day(s)	Hours

Telephone Batting Average

Dials						Contacts				
1	2	3	4	5		1	2	3	4	5
6	7	8	9	10		6	7	8	9	10
11	12	13	14	15		11	12	13	14	15
16	17	18	19	20						
21	22	23	24	25						
26	27	28	29	30		Appointments				
31	32	33	34	35						
36	37	38	39	40		1	2	3	4	5
41	42	43	44	45		6	7	8	9	10
46	47	48	49	50						

No one can stop you from dialing the phone. No one can stop you from asking for the right person. If you will perform the inputs, the outputs will take care of themselves.

If you have been in your territory for a long time and work mainly with existing customers and referrals, set a goal to make three prospecting calls a day to keep yourself sharp and in selling shape.

If you are not getting the sales results you are looking for, it is probably because you are not making enough calls! Refer back to the bottom of Figure 3-4, "Telephone Batting Average," for a simple way to keep track of your productivity.

For many salespeople, their performance chart looks like a series of peaks and valleys. That's because they stop prospecting when business is good. The best time to prospect is when you are "hot," when you need it the least. A confident, expectant attitude has an uncanny positive effect on prospects. The less you seem to need them, the more they want you.

When business is slow and you need new prospects, that slight eagerness is picked up by the prospect, and he tends to draw back.

Make prospecting an activity for all seasons and you will straighten out that performance chart on the high side.

I was approached recently by a young woman who had attended our sales training course and was making an auspicious beginning as a salesperson. She eagerly told me about the number of appointments she had obtained and the sales she was closing.

I asked her how her prospecting techniques were working. An embarrassed look crossed her face and she replied guiltily, "Arnie, I'm so involved with servicing the accounts I've sold and handling the details, I have no time for anything else. I can't even think of prospecting."

I advised her to set aside one hour each day, preferably the first hour, to do nothing but prospect for new business. "Keep calling until you get at least one good prospect," I said, "don't take calls during this time. In this way, you'll keep the pipeline filled while you're taking care of existing business."

Summary

1. Prospecting is the lifeblood of your business. Accept the fact that it has to be done. The more prospects you have, the greater your sales productivity. As a rule of thumb, have three times your monthly sales target in prospective business.
2. Prospecting must be done regularly. Set a schedule and stick to it.
3. Profile the best prospects for what you sell. Classify them as As. Do the same for the Bs and Cs.
4. Set up a call frequency schedule to ensure that your time is allocated effectively.
5. Determine the sources of prospects for your business. Find the directories they are listed in, the associations they belong to, and the publications they read.
6. Your present customers are your best prospects. They are also good sources for referrals.
7. Set up a simple prospecting system using 3 in. x 5 in. cards.
8. Set prospecting goals. Determine how many dials, contacts, and appointments you need to achieve your goals and perform these "inputs."
9. Remember, if you are not getting the sales results you want, it's probably because you are not making enough calls.

Winners do the things that losers don't like to do. Winners don't like to do them either, but they do them anyway.

4
How to Get Appointments on the Telephone

At times I feel that phone prospecting is like sticking your chin out with your hands tied behind your back and daring someone to hit you. You just know eventually someone will.

I really have to discipline myself to prospect on the phone and the longer I delay, the harder it gets.

Even my best clients don't always take my calls. I've got to keep telling myself, it's not personal.

Let's review the steps in the prospecting system:
1. Acknowledge prospecting as the first step in the selling process and the key to your selling success.
2. Establish a prospect profile and classify prospects.
3. Find prospects that fit the profile. (Use directories, old files, present customers, referrals; join associations; and develop a "prospecting awareness.")
4. Set up a recordkeeping and follow-up system.
5. Set prospecting goals.
6. Set up a prospecting schedule.
   We've already covered the first six steps in the previous chapter. You have identified your prospects, classified them by their potential, set up a card system, and developed a prospecting schedule. Now, we will add two final steps to the prospecting system:
7. Prepare a telephone presentation.
8. Keep score of dials, contacts, and appointments and fine tune as required.

Don't schedule anything else during times of the week you will be prospecting. Make an unbreakable date with yourself. Get into the habit of making your prospecting calls at the same time each week.

Do not accept incoming calls while prospecting unless they are urgent. Concentrate on the job at hand.

OK, you are ready to start making calls. What is the best way to get your story across? What happens when the voice on the other end objects, stalls, or gives excuses as to why it cannot see you? How will you handle it?

Effective telephone prospecting needs *planning*, working from a prepared script. You have to be ready for any situation that comes up. The best way to do that is to anticipate. I bet I know what you're thinking. "A script? That's terrible. It's canned. I can't use a script—it cramps my style. I'll sound stilted and unnatural!"

Don't worry, you'll have ample opportunity to be spontaneous and creative. Remember, the prospect plays his role as he sees fit. By knowing what you are going to say and having a track to run on, you will be able to concentrate on what your prospect is saying and how he says it. You will be able to *listen* better.

With practice, you will deliver a presentation that sounds fresh and spontaneous. Program a few "ahs," "you knows," and pauses if you have to.

When was the last long-running stage play you saw? Didn't it seem to you and the audience that the performance was given just for you? Yet the actors were speaking the same words in the exact same way, performance after performance. Using a script will prevent you from getting emotional and saying the wrong things, especially when the prospect is rude or putting pressure on you.

Think of your telephone presentation as a stage play. You are the author, director, and star performer. Unfortunately, the other performer is ad-libbing his role, but you have to control his reponses as much as possible.

In this chapter, you will learn how to get appointments with prospects you have not previously contacted. There are instances when you will be calling referrals, making re-calls, or responding to inquiries. Your script may vary for those types of calls.

Pre-call Preparation

Prepare yourself mentally and physically. Have a goal for dials, contacts, and appointments. Have your score sheet handy.

Check your attitude. Are you ready to call? Are you ready to *win*? Use affirmations and visualization to mentally experience the results you will achieve. Using a mirror on your desk will ensure that your facial gestures and posture are reflecting the enthusiasm and confidence you want to project. Dress for business, even if you are calling from home. Program yourself physically, emotionally, and rationally for this important selling activity.

Have all your materials ready. This should include your prospect cards, customer list, notepaper, account records, pens and pencils, script, "objections handbook," calendar, score sheet, map, and anything else necessary for phone prospecting.

Basic Steps in a Telephone Presentation

The following is an example of the type of script you will use. It begins when the person you have asked to speak with answers the phone.

Step 1: Identify your prospect, yourself, and your company.
Prospect: (answering phone) "Hello."
Salesperson: "Mr. Prospect?"
Prospect: "Yes."
Salesperson: "Mr. Robert Prospect?"
Customer: (coming to life) "Yes, who's this?"
Note: The repetition of the prospect's name using first and last name is used as a preoccupation breaker. It ensures that you have your prospect's complete attention.
Salesperson: "Mr. Prospect, this is John Q. Salesperson with the ABC Courier Company. Does that name ring a bell?"
Customer: "I'm not sure it does. What is this about?"
Salesperson: "Mr. Prospect, ABC is an international courier that offers overnight delivery around the world for your time-sensitive documents."

Step 2: Make a rapport-building statement.
Salesperson: "I've heard a great deal about your firm's international activities and have been looking forward to speaking with you."
or

"We've helped other companies in your industry and perhaps we can be of service to you."

or

"Your company (use name) enjoys a fine reputation, and I've been looking forward to meeting with you to see if we can be of service."

Note: You are attempting to establish a common bond with the prospect at this point. If you have some information about his firm or if you are aware of an event affecting his company, use it.

Customer: "What can I do for you?"

Step 3: Qualify your prospect.

Salesperson: "Mr. Prospect, do you make the decision as to which courier to use for your international work?"

Customer: "Yes."

Salesperson: "Is there anyone else involved in the decision?"

Note: If the person you are talking to is not the decision maker, find out the name of the person who is.

Customer: "Yes, Bill King, our shipping department supervisor is also involved."

Note: The salesperson takes note of this information.

Step 4: Find out the facts.

Note: Ask the questions necessary to determine whether the prospect has a need or application for your services.

Salesperson: "Mr. Prospect, to what countries do you presently ship? What is the frequency? What kind of documents do you ship? How critical is overnight delivery?"

Note: Of course, the prospect's responses will dictate the kinds of questions you will ask. In this step, you are qualifying for *need*.

Step 5: Deliver your sales message.

"Mr. Prospect, ABC courier is small enough to treat every client individually—with a personal touch. You are assured of flexible service to meet your most unusual requirements—and at the right price."

Note: Your selling message should answer the questions, in each prospect's mind: "Why should I see you?" "What's in it for me?" (WIIFM)

Your sales message needs to be "salesy," that is, persuasive with impact. It should promise benefits that whet the prospect's appetite to hear more. Don't clutter your sales message with features.

Step 6: Request an appointment.
"I'd like to show you how we can handle your shipments to your complete satisfaction. Let's get together. How does your calendar look for Monday at 10:00 A.M. or is Tuesday at 3:00 P.M. a better time?"
Note: This is the alternate choice close, giving the prospect a choice of two positive alternatives. Another example is, "Are mornings or afternoons better for you?"
Prospect: "Well, I'm kind of busy right now. Can you send me something in the mail?"

Step 7: Handle the objection.
Salesperson: "I appreciate the value of your time, Mr. Prospect. But literature sometimes raises more questions than it answers. It will take just 18 minutes for me to show you how our service can benefit you. Is Monday morning a good time for you or is Tuesday afternoon better?"
Note: The salesperson was prepared for the prospect's "Send it in the mail" response. The procedure for handling objections on the telephone is:
(a) Acknowledge the objection
"I appreciate the value of your time, Mr. Prospect."
(b) Respond
"Literature sometimes raises more questions than it answers. It will take just eighteen minutes for me to show you how our services can benefit you."
(c) Close
"Is Monday morning a good time for you or is Tuesday afternoon better?"
Customer: "Monday is OK. I can't give you much more than eighteen minutes though."

Step 8.: Confirm the appointment.
Salesperson: "That's fine. Perhaps Bill King would want to be present, also. I'll see you Monday, November _____ at 10:00 A.M. I've marked my calendar. Thank you, Mr. Prospect. Have a good day."

Note: You may want to leave your phone number so the prospect can
reach you.

Let's review the basic steps in a telephone presentation and some
key points.

Developing a Phone Presentation	Key Points
1. Identify your prospect, yourself, and your company.	— Be enthusiastic. — Be clear and concise. — Don't keep your prospect guessing as to what you do. — If you have a difficult name to pronounce, repeat it. Say "sounds like" or use your first name. — If you are not sure of the prospect's name, ask him to please spell it.
2. Make a rapport-building statement.	— Referral (the best). — Favorable comment. — Related event. — Industry knowledge.
3. Qualify your prospect.	— Identify the decision maker. — More than one?
4. Find out the facts.	— Criteria to sell. — Learn more about the company.
5. Deliver your sales message.	— Short and persuasive. — Stress benefits. — Go directly to step 6.
6. Request an appointment.	— State reason. — Use alternate choice. — Assume acceptance.

7. Handle the objection.   ARC:
                              — Acknowledge.
                              — Respond.
                              — Close.

8. Confirm the appointment.   — Restate time, date, your name,
                                and company name. You may
                                want to leave your phone
                                number in case the prospect
                                needs to reach you.

Remember that the goal of the phone call is to get an appointment. If you say too much on the phone, there will be no need for the prospect to see you in person.

Do your real selling face to face.

Objections

Objections are a fact of life. You are going to get them so be prepared. They are knee-jerk reactions to a solicitation, the initial inclination to say "no."

Most phone objections are stalls, put-offs, excuses to get you off the phone. They are called "invalid" objections. They are more emotional than logical and have to be treated as such.

As mentioned, the three-step process for meeting objections is the ARC method.

1. Acknowledge
2. Respond
3. Close

This has to be done quickly and positively, and it has to be followed by a request for an appointment.

There are certain typical objeections that most phone prospectors hear. They are listed below along with the suggested responses. Make a list of the objections you get on the phone and then write the best answers. If you can do this in conjunction with other salespeople in your company, you will get the benefit of choosing from a variety of responses.

When you have finalized your responses to objections, test them in actual phone presentations. Fine tune them until you get them exactly as you want them.

Then set up an "objections handbook." Go to a photo store that sells albums with plastic holders for 4 in. x 6 in. pictures in a flip-up or shingled (overlapping) arrangement. Type each objection on the bottom of a 4 in. x 6 in. sheet so it will project out from the one above. Then type the actual answer or answers above each objection.

Keep your objections handbook next to your script when making calls. When you hear an objection, flip to the appropriate place and presto, there is the answer, exactly as you would like to present it.

After a while, you will memorize the responses and will no longer need to refer to your book. By that time, you will have become a fine prospector and be on your way to success in selling.

Typical Telephone Objections and Responses

"I don't think I'm interested."
"I can understand that Mr./Ms. _____ . It would be presumptuous of me to expect you to be interested until I can show you how you might increase productivity, reduce costs, and save money with our system. We've been able to accomplish this for other companies such as yours. (Mention names if applicable.)

"May I take just twenty-two minutes to explain how we can accomplish this. What's better for you, mornings or afternoons?"

"I think you're wasting your time."
"Mr. _____ , thank you for being so considerate. I appreciate the value of your time, as well as my own, that's why I phoned ahead. What I have to say may be worth thousands of dollars to you and your company.

I believe I can prove it if you can spare twenty-two minutes. Might you have some time on Tuesday morning or perhaps Thursday afternoon?"

"I really don't have the time right now."
"Mr. _____ , I appreciate that you are working on a tight schedule. It's important that you hear this information, and I'd be glad to arrange an appointment at your convenience. Perhaps before 9:00 A.M. or after 5:00 P.M., if that's better? I promise we won't go beyond eighteen minutes. How about 8:45 A.M. tomorrow, and I'll bring the coffee. How do you take yours?" (A little feisty, perhaps. Use your judgment).

"Would you drop the information in the mail?"

"Ms. _____ , I really feel that sending you a brochure would do an injustice to both of us. It may raise more questions than it answers. I could give you a much more meaningful picture of how you may benefit from this system in just eighteen minutes in person. What's better for you, Monday at 10:00 A.M. or Tuesday at 11:00 A.M.?"

"No money in the budget."

"That's perfectly alright, Mr. _____ . In these times, we all need to control expenses. I'd like you to know about the benefits of our system because it has helped other companies such as yours to reduce costs. How is Monday at 10:00 A.M. or Tuesday at 11:00 A.M.?"

"Tell me on the phone."

"Mr. _____ , I want to show you something that will shorten the explanation and save you time. I'd be doing both of us an injustice if I didn't meet with you in person. What is more convenient, Monday at 10:00 A.M. or Tuesday at 11:00 A.M.?

"We're satisfied with our present supplier/equipment/system/service, etc."

"Ms. _____ , I respect your loyalty. All I want to do is to keep you current on the most up-to-date information on _____ . You're *entitled* to this service and there is *no* obligation. It's my job. At the very least, you'll keep your current supplier on his toes."

or

"It's good business to have an alternate source. It keeps everyone on their toes, and you get the benefit of the best service."

Getting through the Secretary's Screen

Secretaries can be difficult to get through, but that is because they have been instructed to carefully guard their bosses' time. Using gimmicks or tricks or trying to power your way into the inner sanctum will work against you more often than not. Annoying a secretary may have a similar effect on the boss.

The best approach is to build rapport with secretaries and to sell them on the benefits their bosses will gain by speaking with you. This may take time, effort, and patience. Show secretaries that you understand their bosses' problems and have a possible solution. After all, secretaries have their bosses' interests at heart. Have a good reason for wanting the appointment.

Humility is a powerful tool. "I've got a problem. I need your help," softens up a lot of hard-boiled people. When you openly acknowledge that someone has the power and position to help you or thwart you, that person is more likely to use that power in a helping way. Most people find it a lot easier to refuse a demand for action than to deny a request for assistance.

It can take a lot of calls to get through to a busy decision maker. It may be an A priority to you, but it's only a C or D to him. Don't let your ego get in the way. Don't take it personally. He is reacting to your "role" as a salesperson. Visualize the end result and keep trying. Some of my best clients are people that were extremely difficult to reach initially. Persistence is a "must" in prospecting.

If you can't get anywhere with the secretary, call early in the morning, after hours, during lunch, or even on weekends, times when the secretary is not likely to be there. You can write and say you will be calling for an appointment, send a mailgram, or try a person-to-person long distance call. Sending pertinent bits of information to your prospect periodically may serve as a door opener. If at first you don't succeed—well, you know the rest.

Things to Remember

Before we leave the subject of getting appointments on the phone, there are some key points that you will want to keep in mind.

1. Telephone prospecting has a high rejection rate. It is not necessarily a reflection on your ability, personality, or product. If you are not getting the number of appointments you would like to, you may not be making enough calls. View each nonappointment call as getting you closer to your goal.

2. *What* you say is not as important as *how* you say it. Friendliness, enthusiasm, a nonthreatening manner, knowledge, determination; these qualities should come through on the phone. If you want the appointment more than the prospect does not want to grant it, you will get a lot of appointments.

3. Adopt an attitude of positive expectancy. Here is what a successful salesperson said about getting through the secretary screen:

"I always find it helpful before I make a call, to *visualize* Mr. Johnson, whatever his position, as a friend of mine, as someone I know personally, who always talks to me and who will welcome hearing from me. It's easy then to imagine that it would be silly for me to telephone this friend of mine and expect his assistant or secretary to keep me from talking to him. Because I know she wouldn't. Now how do you suppose Johnson's friends would ask for him when they talk to his secretary?

"As I said before, I'd say, 'Mr. Johnson please, this is Joe Salesperson,' and nine times out of ten he will pick up the phone a second later."

4. No sales techniques work all the time. To be valid for you, it need only work one more time out of ten than your present approach.

For example, if what you are doing now is getting you two appointments out of ten contacts and you get three appointments using what we have suggested, you have realized a 50 percent increase in productivity.

5. When you get through to the decision maker, make sure your phone presentation is *benefit oriented.* It should answer his unspoken question, "Why should I see you?" Present a realistic benefit early in the interview, preferably in your opening statement.

6. Don't be tempted to stray from your prepared script. If it has proved to be successful, stick with it. You may be getting a bit bored with it, but the prospect who is hearing it for the first time is not. Visualize your little production as a successful, long-running show on Broadway. The financial backers would not permit you to tinker with the dialogue as long as the theater was packed.

7. Practice, practice, practice. Listen to yourself on tape, or watch and listen on videotape. Check your pronunciation, enunciation, pacing, and expression. Put a smile into your voice. Create a desire for your prospect to want to see you.

Remember, nothing worthwhile comes easy. Selling is not a profession for dabblers. It requires courage, commitment, and perseverance. Stick with it. Keep calling. Will you begin Monday at 10:00 A.M. or Tuesday at 11:00 A.M.?

5
Planning—Making Every Call Count

I enjoy the challenge of spontaneously handling what-ever the prospect brings up. It gets my competitive juices flowing.

But I think I've blown a few because I didn't do my homework. There have been times I couldn't think of what questions to ask.

Congratulations! You have an appointment. You have qualified the decision maker, obtained information about the company, and determined that there is an application for what you sell. The date is firm and you are anticipating your meeting with positive expectancy. But have you given any thought to what you are going to do when you get there?

What do you want to accomplish on this call? What is your objective?

These are just a few of the questions that ought to come to mind before making your sales call. The answers to these and other questions should be carefully considered before you get in front of your prospect.

"Hold on," you say, "I'm an experienced hand, and I know my product and my prospect pretty well so I don't need much preparation." You are probably one of those fortunate people who is "good on his feet," thinks quickly, and is rarely flustered or caught off guard. You even look forwrd to the thrill of not knowing what to expect and relish the challenge of confronting the unknown and mastering it.

Generally speaking, a sales call should not be an isolated event. It should be a step in a process that brings you closer to your overall goal, an ongoing client. It should be part of an account strategy.

There are types of selling that require one-call closes, but these are becoming fewer as buyers become more sophisticated and the choice of products grows.

Regardless of what you sell, you want to make every call count. Try to leave as little as possible to chance. Many of us have had the unpleasant experience of having to sit through a lengthy meeting that seemingly had no agenda, plan, or purpose. Prospects get the same feeling from salespeople who make sales calls without proper preparation.

The ability to speak spontaneously and extemporaneously is an enviable talent. Most of us have to be content with carefully anticipating what will happen during the call and diligently preparing ourselves to respond as knowingly and intelligently as we can.

A word of caution to those of you who count on your quick wit and fast footwork to field anything that comes your way. Deals are often won and lost by "inches." If your prospects sense that you haven't really done your homework, they may project this impression to the kind of aftersale service they can expect. They may decide that it would be safer to do business with your more painstaking competitor. Your prospect's time is valuable. You show respect for that time when you prepare properly.

Pre-call planning is a *must*. This applies to phone calls as well as face-to-face meetings. It is natural to pick up the receiver and call without much thought about what may come up or what the objective is. Be ready for incoming calls as well. Have you ever had the experience of receiving a return call from someone you tried to contact days earlier for an appointment, being caught off guard, and blowing it? After you've hung up, you think of all the things you could have said if you were prepared.

Readiness and preparation build confidence and professionalism. Remember, if you don't know where you're going, you may end up somewhere else. It is important to know where you're headed and whether you've won or lost on every sales call.

We recommend the use of a pre-call planner (Figure 5-1) to ensure that you are thoroughly prepared for the call. Although the form is designed primarily for "live" sales calls, it can be used effectively for any type of customer contact, including entertaining. A business lunch is just a specialized form of a sales call. Plan what you want to accomplish in advance even if it is only to strengthen the relationship. Use the pre-call planner when making phone calls, responding to requests for information, or handling complaints.

A sample of the pre-call planner (Figure 5-1) is shown at the end of this chapter. Let's review the steps involved in using the pre-call planner.

1. *Key Data*

   Review your records for key information about the account. What are the important issues you will need to address? If you have no information, get an annual report, sales literature or talk to someone using the product or service. Try to learn what business the prospect is in; who uses his product or service; when, where, and how the product is distributed; and who the competition is.

   Do you have users in the same line of business or with similar applications that you can make references to during your call?

   Reading business and trade magazines and the business section of your daily paper will provide you with information on many companies and industries and can arm you with data that can prove useful in breaking the ice and building rapport.

2. *Key People to See*

   How many people will be present at the meeting? Are they decision makers, decision influencers, or decision implementers? Are there other people in the company you should contact? What are their perspectives and attitudes toward your company and product? What are their individual personality styles? Who is on your side, neutral, or against you? How is the decision made?

3. *Call Objective*

   What do you want to accomplish? State your objective in terms of a specific action that you want your prospect to take as a result of this call. Avoid nebulous or intangible objectives such as "I want him to show interest." Rather, state this in a tangible way such as, "He will come to a demonstration," "He will give me three referrals," "He will contact a user," or "She will authorize a needs analysis." In stating your objective, consider how the prospect will benefit by taking the action you are recommending. Become prospect or audience oriented. A good way to state your objective is as follows:

   If I can persuade them that _____ (description of offering) will help them _____ (benefit), then they will _____ (recommended action).

Example:

If I can persuade them that *our portable Expo Plus Display Unit* (description of offering) will help them *attract more customers to their exhibit* (benefit), then they will *visit our showroom for a demonstration* (recommended action). Your call objective should be realistic and attainable.

4. *Opener*

You want to establish a friendly, nonthreatening climate and gain your prospect's interest and attention. You may refer to a prior meeting or conversation or a current event of general interest. If this is your first meeting, you might bring up something relevant to the prospect or his company. It could be as simple as a complimentary comment on the building or the office decor. There is no shame in planning your opening remarks so that you enter your prospect's world in a way that appeals to him. We are not all so glib and comfortable socially that we can accomplish the opening without prior preparation.

After establishing a rapport, you state the purpose of your call, indicate a potential general benefit for the prospect, and earn the right to ask questions.

5. *Questions*

This is the key to selling. You don't know how you can help your prospects until you know what their needs are. Intelligent questions are a clear indication to your prospects that you know your business and theirs, too. *Prepare your important questions in advance and write them down so you don't forget them.* What do you need to know to make an effective presentation? What is the definite need, the "hot button," the dominant buying motive that will make a prospect want to buy?

6. *Features and Benefits*

A feature is defined as a prominent characteristic or part of your product or service. It describes what the product is, what it does, how it works. A feature is a fact.

A benefit is how the feature will help the prospect, the ways in which the prospect will gain from using the feature. Benefits can be tangible or intangible.

Example:

Feature: This book has a chapter entitled "How To Get Appointments on the Telephone."

Tangible Benefit: It will enable you to get more appointments, increasing your sales and earnings.

Intangible Benefit: You will feel more confident and secure knowing that you are doing the right things and doing them right!

In planning your sales call, list the features you are most likely to present and how they will benefit your prospect. Try to be as specific as possible in relating these benefits to the person.

How can you prove to your prospects that they will realize the same benefits you've just described? Use proofs.

Proofs include demonstrations, samples, testimonial letters, results of tests or research studies, product specifications, and case histories. Having your prospects talk with satisfied customers is an excellent way to prove the credibility of your claims.

7. *Anticipated Objections*

What objections is your prospect likely to raise? Write them down, and then write down how you will respond. Being prepared to take on whatever your prospect offers will give you confidence and a positive attitude. If you are sure an objection will be raised, you can minimize it by bringing it up yourself. Role play the objection with a colleague to ensure that you are answering the objection clearly and convincingly.

8. *Close*

How will you ask for the action specified in your objective? What words, phrases, or sentences will you use? Suppose you get turned down the first time, how will you ask a second or third time if necessary? Many salespeople have trouble asking for action (getting commitment). Choosing the right words and phrases is a lot easier when you are calm and collected than in the heat of battle where emotions, especially yours, might be high.

Prepare several closes in writing, in advance.

9. *Appropriate Sales Aids*

What materials do you need? Do you have a presentation binder, audiovisuals, handouts, product literature, and testimonials? What about order blanks, calculator, sales promotion material? It may sound repetitious, but thinking about these things in advance will ensure that you have the important materials you need with you.

10. *Special Competitive Factors*
    Is competition strongly entrenched in this account? Is the competition offering a special program or new features, or do your competitor and your prospect have an unusual relationship (such as when your competitor is a customer of your prospect)? These factors may influence how you conduct the sales call.

11. *Results*
    After the call, write down the results. Did you achieve your call objective? If not, why? What went well and what did not? Where are the opportunities for improvement?

    What is your action plan for the account? What do you plan to do next and when?

    File the planner for use on your next call.

    Don't be tempted to limit your pre-call planning to mental preparation. Certainly, just thinking through these steps in advance is better than doing nothing. However, writing crystallizes thought, and crystallized thought motivates action! Most of us can think more clearly and sort out alternatives better when we get our thoughts down in black and white. It is easier to compare and prioritize items when they are in writing. One idea seems to trigger another. Thoughts in the mind might be clear and uncluttered at the moment, but can you be sure you will enjoy the same lucidity and recall at a later time? Ideas are fleeting; capture them on paper.

    Write a pre-call planner for every call. Keep blanks in your car and attache case and if you absolutely don't have the time to fill one out on a particular call, take a few moments and scan it before going in. Make sure you have a specific objective for every call (including phone calls). You will become more goal oriented and accomplish more with less effort. Intelligent pre-call planning will increase the effectiveness of every call you make.

Figure 5-1
Pre-Call Planner

Account Name: _____   Date: _____

1. Key Data: _____

_____

_____

_____

2. Key People to See:

Name: _____   Title/Function: _____

Name: _____   Title/Function: _____

Name: _____   Title/Function: _____

DM = Decision maker   DI = Decision influencer
DP = Decision implementer   CI = Center influence

3. Call Objective: (What action should prospect take?)

_____

_____

_____

_____

4. Opener: (Build rapport; gain interest and attention.)

_____

_____

_____

5. Questions: _____

_____

_____

_____

6. Features and Benefits:

Features	Benefits	Proof

7. Anticipated Objections:

Objections	Response

8. Close: (List three closing questions or statements you will use to get agreement on the action stated in your call objective.)

_____

_____

_____

9. Appropriate Sales Aids:

Brochures	Testimonials	Presentation kit
Audiovisuals	Proofs	Other

_____

_____

10. Special Competitive Factors: _____

_____

_____

11. Results:

_____

_____

_____

6
Bring on the Warm Fuzzies and Communicate

I used to think that the key to selling was getting a lot of prospects and aggressively presenting the product. I guess I was focusing on my needs instead of their's.

It's amazing what another person's voice, intonations, and body movements can tell you if you're looking for them. Why didn't I see them before?

It's real tough to get into an account where my competitor is well liked. It seems that feelings and emotions play a bigger part in purchasing than I thought.

Would you buy something from someone you did not trust, someone who was intimidating or threatening, who made you feel uncomfortable? Not unless they made you an offer you couldn't refuse. How about someone who put you at ease, created a relaxed atmosphere, and who seemed to be genuinely concerned with meeting your needs? All things being equal, you would be more apt to respond favorably in the second situation.

People buy for two primary reasons or needs. First, they have a "task" or rational need for a product or service. You need a haircut and go to the barber. That is a logical or rational reason for "buying."

However, you just don't go to *any* barber or hairdresser. You go to one that welcomes you warmly, addresses you by your first name, and gives you lots of PI (personal identity). After he's through cutting your hair, he concludes with "OK handsome, the ladies better beware." You leave the shop with a slight glow, feeling a bit better about yourself.

The barber has satisfied the second need, the *emotional* or *psychological* needs you have for acceptance, respect, and recognition. You have gotten your "strokes" from the barber. In your own mind, you rationalize that the real reason you use him is because he does a good job of styling your hair. This may be true, but there are probably other barbers that could do an equally good job. This barber, a "natural" salesperson, will keep you as a customer because he is satisfying you on both rational and emotional levels.

People prefer to deal with salespeople who they like, feel comfortable with, believe in, and who support the positive image they have of themselves.

Your ability to satisfy the emotional or personality needs of your prospects and customers in addition to meeting their task or rational needs will tip the scale in your favor when the competition is breathing down your neck. The stronger the relationship you have with your customer, the *less important price becomes.*

It bears repeating. The stronger the relationship you have with your customer, the less important *price* becomes.

How can you as a professional salesperson create a positive selling climate in which your offering has the best chance of being favorably received?

There are four basic rules for setting the proper milieu:
1. Build trust and rapport.
2. Eliminate threat and defensiveness.
3. Communicate congruently.
4. Match your own communicating style to your prospect's style.

1. *Build Trust and Rapport*
   The word rapport comes from the French word *rapporter*, to bring back. Rapport is the element that brings customers back into your "fold" time and time again. You build rapport when you show a genuine interest and understanding of the other person, not only as a customer, but as a unique individual.

   Think about your five best customers. How much do you know about them? What kind of families do they have, where do they live, what are their interests and hobbies, political preferences, favorite books, life experiences, goals and expectations? If you can't answer these questions, can you really build a personal relationship with them?

To truly understand how your prospects feel, you must get into their worlds. How can you create affinity and a common bond if you don't know anything about the other person? How do you get this information? Ask.

Most people enjoy talking about themselves, especially if they know they will not be judged or evaluated. It is surprising how often people will reveal personal aspects of their lives to a complete stranger. One of the reasons this occurs is because it is not easy to find someone who will listen in an empathetic, nonjudgmental manner. The more you know about a person, the more opportunities there are for you to build a relationship.

If being interested in others does not come naturally to you, you will have to make it a consciously developed skill. Remember, we sell to people, not companies. I have never had four walls, a roof, or a factory give me business. Only people can sign orders.

Appropriate dress, a pleasant demeanor, promptness, courtesy, a ready smile, neatness, good grooming, a low-key (somewhat tentative) approach (if you are meeting for the first time), and a predetermined and sincere effort to like the other person will help build trust and rapport. These characteristics are basic to selling, but it is surprising how often they are ignored.

Knowing your product, your company's policies and programs, your customer's business, your customer's customers, the industry and being well prepared for the call are all important trust builders. Sincerity and a pleasing personality are pluses, but there is no substitute for knowing your business.

Complimenting your prospect with sincere, genuine strokes (and avoiding plastic ones) is a powerful relationship builder. We all like to receive positive strokes to have others acknowledge us and confirm our strengths.

Everyone needs strokes to maintain a sound emotional balance. Psychologists tell us that each of us has an internal "stroke counter," that tallies up the strokes we get each day until our personal quota has been satisfied. If we fall short, we actively seek strokes until that quota is met.

Interestingly enough, if we can't get positive strokes (warm fuzzies), we will subliminally opt for negative strokes (cold pricklies). Because a stroke is a unit of recognition, either a positive or negative stroke is better than no stroke at all. Children will often "act up," or even do something destructive to get their parents' attention if they can not get it any other way.

Another effective method to build rapport is to get in sync with your prospect through voice matching and body mirroring. To voice match, you adjust your tone, pacing, volume, and rate of speech to that of your prospect. If your prospect speaks slowly or pauses a lot, you do the same.

Body mirroring is reflecting the other person's posture and nonverbal signs with your own. If the prospect's posture is rigid and formal, you should sit upright. If he relaxes in his chair, assume a more relaxed demeanor.

Note that when matching and mirroring, the changes in your voice and posture are subtle and not obvious to the prospect on a conscious level. Nevertheless, the effect is to indicate to the prospect that "we're alike—you can trust me."

Another form of matching is adjusting your breathing rate to that of the other person. People breathe from different parts of their body and in different ways. It is another technique of getting in step with the other person.

It is obvious from the above that to properly match and mirror, you need to be observing and listening intently, focusing your attention on your prospect instead of yourself.

Listen with your eyes as well as your ears. Listen for feeling as well as content. Try to mentally summarize the main points. Listen to the words and expressions your prospect uses, then adroitly weave them into your own conversation. Listen without judgment or evaluation, it tells your prospects that you understand and accept their right to their views. Don't focus on what you are going to say—you might miss a key point. If you are unsure of a point, get clarification by saying, "Mr. Prospect, let me see if I understand you. Is what you are saying . . .?"

To clarify a statement, start with, "Is it fair to say that . . .?"

Listen attentively and actively, sprinkling applause such as, "That's interesting," "Really?," "Could you expand on that?," or "Wow!"

Some Don'ts:
A. Don't knock the competition.
B. Don't put down other individuals or departments in your own company who you feel have let you down.
C. Don't divulge confidential information gained from other customers.
D. Don't ever forget your business relationship no matter how friendly you become with customers.
E. Don't overuse expressions such as:
I'm sure you'll agree.
I'm sure you won't mind.
I'm sure you'll like.
F. Don't get sloppy or careless in your dealings because of familiarity. Keep the relationship business oriented.
G. Don't discuss—or remain neutral on—controversial subjects such as religion, politics, and sex.

Remember, your customer is someone else's prospect. Your competition is putting their best foot forward to sell him.

Perhaps this definition of a friend can help you establish the type of relationship you should foster with your customers. "I like my friend because when I'm with him, I like *me* better."

If your customers like *themselves* better when they are with you, you will build a loyal and profitable client base.

2. *Eliminate Threat and Defensiveness*
Many people feel threatened in a selling situation. They feel they may be pressured to buy, pay too much, make a foolish decision, waste their time, or receive poor aftersale service. What is threatened is the buyer's *self-image*.

Each of us has a mental picture of the kind of person we are or how we would like to be viewed by others. A prospect who values friendship wants the salesperson to recognize and acknowledge that trait. Another who is security oriented needs to have safety, reliability, and dependability stressed. Achiever types want to feel that their need to "be number one" can be satisfied by your offering (which should promise them the uniqueness and status they seek). Make an effort to identify and support the other's self-image in the way you give your presentation.

Don't let your ego get in the way. Belittling a prospect's present system or product to make your offering more attractive is a sure way to get his defenses up and create a show-me attitude.

Establishing credibility by presenting evidence of past successes is fine, but the goal should be to deal with the prospects' concerns about your ability to solve their problems, not to build yourself up.

Some prospects seem to demand a disproportionate amount of your time relative to the amount of business they have to offer. It's not always easy to be diplomatic about making them aware of this, but becoming cavalier and informing them how busy you are is not the best way. Being up-front and honest in how much of your time they can reasonably expect and why is a better way.

Don't state your opinion as if it's fact. Use phrases such as "in my opinion," "in my view," "it is our experience," and "we believe."

Don't ascribe your own value system or motivations to your prospects. They may buy or not buy for reasons very much different than yours. Deal from their perspectives.

Make your prospects comfortable and relaxed. You are there to help them. Avoid leading questions or manipulative statements such as, "I'm sure you want to have the latest model, don't you?" Ask open-ended questions that permit a wide latitude in response. Avoid directive or yes/no questions early in the interview. Don't make exorbitant claims about your offerings. Be able to back up what you say with proof. Use testimonials, show examples of your work, or demonstrate your product's benefits to your prospects.

Allow prospects to be candid, to express misgivings about your offering, to raise objections, and to ask pointed questions without argument. Rather than rebut or defend your position, use reflective or mirroring statements that show acceptance and understanding of a customer's position. Never take an adversarial position. Instead, get on the same side as the buyer. A selling situation should pit buyer and seller against a problem, not each other.

3. *Communicate Congruently*
"What you are speaks so loudly I can't hear what you're saying."

A noted communications researcher found that in face-to-face communications between two people, the receiver attributes meaning to the sender's message by evaluation in three areas:

Verbal	(words)
Paraverbal	(tone, expression, volume, pacing)
Nonverbal	(physical behavior and general appearance)

The contribution to the meaning of a message by each area was discovered to be as follows:

Verbal	7%
Paraverbal	38%
Nonverbal	55%

What this says is that the words we use and how we say them are not nearly as important as our appearance, expression, gestures, body language, and physical presence.

If there is a conflict in the receiver's mind between what we're saying and the nonverbal message we're sending, the receiver will believe the nonverbal message.

Everything about you tells a story. Certainly your dress and grooming are very critical. They create a sensory impact on the prospect that produces an immediate impression. It is vital that this impression be as positive as possible. People form an opinion of you in the first thirty seconds and spend the next thirty minutes justifying it. You never get a second chance to make a good first impression.

Give careful consideration to your wardrobe. Don't be like a salesperson I knew who boasted, "I have a suit for every day in the week—and I'm wearing it." Unfortunately, he looked it. There is no one better deserving of an investment from you than yourself. Don't wait to become successful to dress successfully. You've got to pay the price up-front to reap the rewards down the line. Put the "act as if" principle to work immediately by acting as if you are already successful by dressing and acting the part. Nonverbal behavior contributes more than half of the message you are getting across. There is no excuse for not being professionally attired. None! If you need help in selecting your wardrobe, go to a good clothing store in your area and explain to the manager the type of image you want to project.

Other aspects of your presence are also part of the total impression you make. These include your voice, manners, diction, vocabulary, posture, facial gestures, attache case, portfolio, brochures, presentation materials, samples, writing pad, pen, and car. Even your pauses contribute meaning.

Be sure everything about you tells a consistent story—the story of a dedicated professional.

There should be a congruency about what you say, how you say it, and your physical behavior while saying it. When you use words like "exciting," "dynamic," "innovative," "slow," "out-of-date," or "difficult," make sure that the expression in your voice as well as your body reflects the real meaning you want to convey. When you say "dynamic," act "dynamic!" and when you say slow, act "s-l-o-w."

Be alert to the paraverbal and nonverbal cues given by your prospects. There may be a contradiction in what they say and how they say it. Prospects who say they will consider your services for their next project without conviction or appropriate body language may really be saying that they are not interested. Prospects communicate on all levels, also. If the words and nonverbal behavior don't match, trust the nonverbal behavior.

4. *Match Your Own Communicating Style to Your Prospect's Style*
Often it's not *what* is said but *how* it's said that causes problems in communication. We tend to favor people who communicate in a way similar to our own, whose style matches ours.

Carl Jung, the famed Swiss psychologist, discovered four fundamental styles that people use to communicate (Jung 1923). They are:
(a) *The Intuitor Style*—Characterized by long-range thinking, creative ideas, theory, working in the abstract, attempting to link seemingly unrelated events and discoveries into a universal theme, originality, and imagination.

Intuitors are found working in architecture, science, writing, directing, art and music, engineering, city planning, the creative side of advertising, corporate planning, and as "idea people."
(b) *The Feeler Style*—Communicating through feelings and intuition, strong people orientation featuring empathy and sensitivity to others

as well as oneself and to the environment, high sensory acuity, emphasis on relationship building to gain outcomes.

Feelers are nurses, secretaries, psychologists, teachers, psychiatrists, counselors, hairdressers, decorators, entertainers, authors, dramatists, social workers, retailers, and real estate people. They work in personnel, human resource development and training, and religious and philanthopic organizations.

(c) *The Thinker Style*—Heavy emphasis on logic, rationality, order, facts, objective thinking, problem solving, weighing alternatives, analysis, and deductive reasoning.

Thinkers are accountants, lawyers, systems people, time and motion people, engineers, researchers, economists, referees, executives, technicians, technical salespeople, controllers, financial people, dentists, professors, data processing personnel, and actuaries.

(d) *The Sensor Style*—Action and results oriented, pragmatic, responsive, driving, competitive. Sensors like to deal with things they can see, hear, and touch. They live in the "now."

Sensors are entrepreneurs, salespeople, construction workers, pilots, bankers, professional athletes, marketing executives, wholesalers, physicians, investors, military strategists, politicians, and business people.

Everyone is a blend of all four styles, but usually one style predominates or is the primary communicating style.

If you are dealing with a primary intuitor, you stress creativity, the "big picture," how your product or program fits into the larger scheme of things. Intuitors are futuristic in their thinking and are not overly concerned by short-run solutions.

The primary "feeler" prefers dealing on a personal level, getting to know and understand the people he comes in contact with. Feelers are "read-between-the-lines" people. Don't be overly factual. Anecdotes, informality, and humor work well here. Feelers often act on intuition and "gut" feelings. Work hard on building a rapport and establishing a close one-to-one relationship.

When presenting to a "thinker," make sure you have your facts straight and ample proof sources to back up your claims. Make your presentations in an objective, analytic style and offer several alternatives. Thinkers do not buy based on the enthusiasm and charisma of the salesperson. Be logical and low key.

The "sensor" wants to know the essentials, the bottom line. Streamlined presentations that do not offer too many alternatives and that have a sense of urgency appeal to the primary sensor. Don't be too conceptual or theoretical. Sensors live in the present and are not overly concerned about long-range effects or past events. Sensors are action oriented and need to feel that they are winners. Show sensors how they will personally gain, beat competition, win an award, or gain recognition by buying your product or service.

To maximize your communication with another, you must bend your own style to match his. Each of us is the center of our own universe. In our own minds, the world we live in revolves around us. If we want to establish a common bond with another person, we must be able to step into his world and see it from his viewpoint.

You bring on the warm fuzzies when you treat your prospects as individuals, listen nonjudgmentally, support the positive image they have of themselves, and enable them to like themselves better.

7
Sellin' Ain't Tellin'—It's Askin'

The reason I'm in selling is because I like being on center stage, making presentations, telling the prospect what's good for him. It's hard for me to shut up and listen.

Isn't it my job to fill in the silences?

If I take too much time asking questions, they won't listen to my story.

Questioning is the most important part of the selling process. If you do a good job in this step, your prospects will often tell you how they want to be sold.

Unfortunately, it is the part that most salespeople shortchange. Perhaps it's because in questioning, the prospect is doing most of the talking. Salespeople have been conditioned to do just the opposite. Selling folklore is full of tales about spellbinding speakers who captivate the buyer into a sale with their charisma and charm.

This isn't to knock charisma and charm. But to use them most effectively, they must be directed toward the real needs of the prospect. The only way to determine these needs is to ask questions (lots of them) and then shut up and listen!

Questioning is used in every step of the selling process. Here are some of the reasons we ask questions:

Why ask questions?
— To get information
— To verify information
— To qualify the prospect (prospect vs. suspect)
— To get the prospect involved

— To learn more about the prospect's personality style
— To show interest in our prospect
— To get appointments
— To find the decision maker
— To check the prospect's reaction to our presentation
— To counter objections
— To clarify unclear statements
— To demonstrate our knowledge of the customer's business
— To get prospects to focus on specific areas
— To get referrals
— To get commitment (closing)

When you are asking questions in a purposeful manner, you are in control of the interview.

As a rule of thumb, on an initial sales call, the prospect should be doing 70 percent of the talking to the salesperson's 30 percent.

· Don't be in a hurry to make a presentation until you are sure why the prospect will buy and that you can deliver that "why." If you leave a sales call uncertain of why a prospect should buy your product or service, you can bet that he is even more uncertain. You have not done a good job of uncovering his real needs. Don't be like the street peddlers on New York City's Fifth Avenue who spread their wares out on the sidewalk and beckon the onlookers to "pick out something you like."

Some salespeople sell by throwing out a bunch of features and benefits, hoping that one or two of them will appeal to the prospect.

What we're talking about in this chapter is the "needs" approach to selling, that is, determining the prospect's needs and then selling to them.

Questioning is not an inquisition
Prospects do not want to feel that they are on the witness stand with a district attorney firing questions at them. The questioning process is interactive. The salesperson provides feedback as well as information during the exchange.

Some prospects will want you to tell them something about your offering before you can start asking questions. Accommodate them but only in a broad, general way. Provide just enough information to satisfy the prospect's curiosity. Suggest that there are potential benefits that

other companies or individuals in a similar business or situation have realized from your product. In this way, you earn the right to ask questions. You might lead into your questioning step this way:
"Mr. Prospect, several of my clients in similar financial circumstances have benefitted from our investment program. However, each case is different and in order for me to determine just how you might benefit from our service, I'll need to ask you a few questions. Is that OK?"

There are three types of questions:
1. open
2. closed
3. reflective

Open questions are questions that cannot easily be answered by one word and never by yes or no. They give the prospect lots of room to talk broadly and expansively. They begin with words such as who, what, where, when, why, and how. Rudyard Kipling (1912) said of them, "I keep six honest serving-men;
(They taught me all I knew)
Their names are What and Why and When/And How and Where and Who."

Examples of open questions are:
"What are your responsibilities in this department?"
"How do you process your orders?"
"When must the shipment arrive?"
"Where are your branches located?"
"What kind of results are you getting with your present equipment?"

Open questions are not threatening and are used in the beginning of the interview to get your prospect talking.

Closed questions are used to direct the prospect's response to areas of agreement usually resulting in a one word answer such as yes or no. Closed questions often begin with "Do you," "Will you," "Can you," "Is it," "Isn't it," "Would you," and "Did you." These questions serve as effective trial closes and also help get the prospect's agreement on a specific point.
Examples:
"Isn't this a beautiful reproduction?"
"Shall we ship it to your home?"

"Would you like to see a demonstration?"
"Can you see how this new model will improve productivity?"
"Do you make the decision concerning menswear purchases?"

Closed questions are directive and therefore more threatening to a prospect. They require a yes/no response. They should be used discreetly, especially early in the interview.

Reflective questions seek clarification or a confirmation of understanding. You use your own words to "reflect" back what you understand the prospect to say or mean. They begin with phrases such as: "If I understand you correctly . . .," "Is what you're saying . . .," "Is it fair to say . . .," and "Could you tell me a little more about that?"
   Examples:
"If I understand you correctly, you feel you should be getting more out of your present system?"
"Are you saying that portability and flexibility are of prime concern to you?"
"Is is fair to say that you are open to new ideas if we can stay within your budget?"

Although reflective-type questions are technically "closed" questions and could be answered with a yes or no, the way in which they are phrased and spoken warrants a more detailed response. Using reflective responses is a good way to show your prospects that you are listening and are interested in what they are saying.

The Three Steps of Questioning

There are three steps in the questioning process. They are qualifying, identifying needs, and intensifying needs.

Step 1: *Qualifying.*

Qualifying is determining if your "suspect" meets the criteria to qualify as a prospect.

   Your time is valuable. Before investing a great deal of it on a potential buyer, you need to satisfy yourself that if you can meet his needs and produce the desired results, he *can* and *will* buy—now!

   There are specific criteria that determine whether you have a prospect.

   Decision making. Can this person make a buying commitment? If not, can he strongly influence the buying decision? How will the decision be made? Who else do you need to involve in the selling process?

Too often we assume that the person we are talking to is the decision maker only to find after investing time and effort that there are others who influence or actually make the decision. It is important to find this information out early in the selling process and involve *all* individuals who can influence the decision.

Need. Is there a recognizable and acknowledged need for your product or service—that is recognized and acknowledged by the prospect? What are his buying criteria? What specifically do you need to convince him of in order to get the business?

Money. Does the prospect have a budget? Can he get the financing and is he willing to make the investment necessary to buy your product or service? Before you go too far down the line, get a preliminary commitment on the investment required. Too many salespeople are reluctant to bring this up early, and as a result, find out after much time and effort that the price is far out of the prospect's reach.

If it is difficult to quote a price without gathering a lot of data, then talk in price "ranges." Satisfy yourself that if you can meet his needs, he can and will make the necessary investment.

Time. When will the prospect take action? Within thirty days? Three months? Six months? Two years? Establish a decision time frame. You will certainly react differently to a deal that will be decided in thirty days as opposed to six months. A fair question to ask is, "Mr. Prospect, if we can meet your requirements and stay within the investment guidelines we discussed, when would you want to get started?"

Competition. Can your product or service best satisfy the prospect's need? Does competition have a better or equal solution at a lower price? Can you compete realistically on this deal?

Who is the competition? Assume there will be competition on every deal, even if nothing is mentioned. Try to anticipate what they have told the prospect. Ask if he has spoken to other vendors. You might be able to get some clues by the kinds of questions he puts to you. There may be instances where the competition is not a competing company but rather an alternative use of the investment required. This is good information to have because you may have to justify your offering in terms of the return on your investment as compared to investing in an advertising program, additional salespeople, or a new wing to the building.

Hidden factors. Are there factors not easily uncovered such as an outside consultant with strong influence, a competitor who is a customer of your prospect or who is a close friend or relative? Cover all the bases in qualifying. Before you submit a proposal, make a presentation or give a demonstration, have a clear understanding of what is needed to close the sale. Be convinced in your own mind that your offering can supply the solution and can give greater value than the competition's.

If these criteria cannot be met in your own mind, decide if it is worthwhile to continue.

You can't sell everyone, nor can you be all things to all people. The smart salesperson knows when to walk away from a deal. Invest your emotional and physical energy where it has the biggest payoff.

Here is a quick summary of the qualifying step. Before moving further in the selling process you need to satisfy yourself on the following points:

• The person(s) you are talking to can and will make a buying decision.
• There is an identified need.
• The prospect is able and willing to make the necessary investment.
• The decision will be made in a reasonable time frame.
• You are competitive in terms of the investment required.
• There are no hidden factors that will influence the sale.

Step 2. *Identifying Needs.*
In this step, we use *fact-finding questions* to uncover possible needs and dissatisfactions and *problem-building* questions to measure a prospect's reaction to these possible needs.

Fact-Finding Questions
Fact-finding questions are used to uncover possible needs, wants, dissatisfaction, problems, or pain that the prospect is experiencing. Each fact-finding question has a purpose—to identify an area of need or opportunity for improvement. The more knowledge you have of your prospect's business or application, the better prepared you are, the better your questions will be.

In the fact-finding stage you should be doing just that—getting facts. Don't try to do any selling here or give too much information.

Even if you uncover a problem area that you can meet, keep on asking questions. You may uncover a stronger need for your offering.

The following example shows a video equipment salesperson questioning a buyer.

Salesperson: (fact-finding) "Do you do any in-house productions?"

Buyer: "Yes, we do."

Salesperson: (fact-finding) "What type of work do you do?"

Buyer: "We occasionally produce a training film for our manufacturing people when we install a new piece of machinery."

Salesperson: (problem-building) "How do you feel about the quality you're getting from your present camera?"

Buyer: "Well, it could be better. The lighting in the factory is not ideal and as you know, this is an old model."

(Note: The salesperson has uncovered an indefinite need and could start to intensify the need. However, he continues to ask questions, probing to see if there are other needs that might present even better opportunities.)

Salesperson: (fact-finding) "What other uses of video do you have?"

Buyer: "We use outside production houses to make videos for our salespeople to use in their presentations."

Salesperson: "How many salespeople do you have?"

Buyer: "About 150 in our domestic operation."

Salesperson: (fact-finding) "What equipment are they using for playback?"

Buyer: "They rent the equipment locally in most cases. We only have a few VCRs."

Salesperson: (problem-building) "Are they always able to get the equipment when they need it?"

Buyer: "Frankly, that does present some difficulties, especially in areas where there is no local dealer. We've been thinking about providing our salespeople with their own units. We want to encourage them to make more presentations."

(Note: The salesperson, by continuing to fact find, has now uncovered a need for 150 portable units, sales value $150,000, in addition to the camera sale he uncovered previously.)

When fact-finding, write the information down. Here is where you put your listening skills to work. Listen for *feeling* as well as *content.* Get the bigger picture of what is said, listen for ideas first, details second. Reflect for clarity and understanding.

Be careful about asking your prospect what he does not like about his present method or supplier. Chances are, you won't get a true answer until he is really comfortable with you. Build trust and rapport before asking confidential questions.

A better way to find out how a prospect feels about his present method is to ask indirectly:
"What would you like to be getting from your present service you're not getting now?" or "If you could design a system from the ground up, what would it look like?"

Examples of general fact-finding questions are:
- What are your responsibilities here at ABC Corporation?
- How do you handle this now?
- What do you like about your present system?
- What information would you like to be getting that you're not getting now?
- How long have you been in this job?
- What is your background?
- What do you look for in a vendor?
- What are your short-term (and long-term) objectives?

Problem-Building Questions
After you have asked enough fact-finding questions, you will want to explore the areas of possible dissatisfaction by asking "problem-building questions." Problem-building questions are used to determine if the prospect views these areas as problems and to what extent. Salespeople see needs faster than prospects. We have a purpose. We are problem seekers. We know our product, and we are looking for possible needs. At this point, the salesperson sees a possible need and attempts to learn if the prospect does also.

Examples of problem-building questions are:
- Does forty-eight hour turn around meet your needs?
- Is the color quality of this print satisfactory?
- Do some of your personnel find it difficult to carry this unit into a prospect's office?
- Are you experiencing excessive dropouts with your present videotape?

Often, fact-finding and problem-building questions are linked together. For example, the fact-finding question might be:
"Do you ever have the need to send the same message to all your branches simultaneously?"

Answer: "Yes, this happens when we have price changes or new programs."
Problem-building question: "Do you ever find that certain branches are getting this information late?"
The way prospects respond to problem-building questions gives us a clue as to how they view the problem and whether it is worth pursuing or "intensifying."

For example, in response to the question, "Do you find that certain branches are getting this information late?", the prospect may respond in either of two ways:
(a) "Yes, but it doesn't make much difference because the branches affected are the smaller ones and are not as sensitive to price changes."
or
(b) "Yes, occasionally we are rushed and some of our branches are delayed in getting the information. They get pretty upset when that happens."

Response (a) indicates that the need is weak and the prospect probably won't act on it. Response (b) indicates that the need is stronger and is worthwhile for the salesperson to pursue. But even this need requires intensification before a presentation is justified.

Definite vs. Indefinite Needs
Before moving into the intensification stage of the questioning process, we need to understand that needs are of varying strengths.

At this very moment you probably have a number of needs that you would like to satisfy. Perhaps you would like a new car, a condo at the beach, a cabin in the mountains, new carpeting and furniture, a compact disc player, a theater subscription, a vacation in Europe, a larger office, a new jogging outfit, tennis racquet or golf clubs, a new suit, dress, attache case—the list is endless.

However, you will act on very few, if any, of these needs immediately. They exist, and you may think of them from time to time, but they are vague, unclear, *indefinite*, and you don't view them as critical. There is no sense of urgency about them. For you to take action, they would have to be intensified, transformed into concrete, time-specific, clear, definite needs.

That is what the questioning process is all about. Uncovering possible problem areas, testing to see if the prospect identifies the problem as a need, then intensifying the need to create a sense of urgency and a desire to have the need satisfied. Questioning involves taking the need out of the vague, unclear, indefinite area and transforming it into a specific, clear, definite reason for taking action.

Step 3. *Intensifying Needs.*
It has been said that we don't necessarily act on what we need, but rather on what we want.

If you accept this, than the intensification step is where needs are converted into wants—and wants into buying action. Two types of questions are used in the intensification step: ramification questions and payoff questions.

Ramification Questions
Ramification questions project the possible consequences of indefinite needs and get the prospect to recognize that he has a "serious" problem or is missing a real opportunity.

The vague, indefinite need is transformed into a definite, recognizable (recognized by your prospect) need.

People learn to live with problems and don't necessarily focus on the real effect of a problem until there is a crisis. The intensification step in the questioning process attempts to get the prospect to see through the problem to all its possible ramifications.

For example, if the brakes on your car began to squeak, but there were no other signs that they were beginning to fail, you might let the needed repairs slide. On the other hand, if a qualified service technician points out that you could be exposing yourself to danger unless you have the brakes repaired immediately, you would be much more likely to have the car serviced.

Payoff Questions
Payoff questions shift the prospect's attention from the problem and its ramifications to the solution you can offer. Payoff questions suggest the positive effects of your offering and arouse a desire in the prospect's mind to hear your solution.

The purpose of payoff questions is to get the prospect to want to learn about your solution.

Examples of payoff questions are:
- If I could get your package to your destination before 11:00 A.M. the next day with proof of delivery, would that solve your problem?
- If we could give you better quality prints in less time and at lower cost, would you give us a try on your next project?
- How do you feel about a modular, portable display unit that anyone could set up and take down in less than two minutes?
- In light of what you've told us, if we could improve your order entry procedure and give you faster and more accurate data, would you seriously consider our system?

Now let's go back to the little scenario we gave before and see how ramification and payoff questions come into play. Notice how the salesperson follows up after his problem-building questions and projects the negative consequences of the problem.

Salesperson (fact-finding question): "Do you ever have the need to send the same message to all your branches simultaneously?"

Prospect: "Yes, that happens when we have price changes or new programs."

Salesperson (problem-building question): "Do you ever find that certain branches are getting this information late?"

Prospect: "Yes, occasionally we are rushed and some of our branches are delayed in getting the information. They get pretty upset when that happens."

Salesperson (ramification question): "What happens when a branch is not notified about these price changes or programs in time and customers inquire?"

Prospect: "Well, it causes difficulties. Customers aren't too happy."

Salesperson (clarifying vague response): "When you say 'not too happy,' what do you mean?"

Prospect: "Well, they may walk out of the store."

Salesperson (clarifying further): "And . . ."

Prospect: "Well, we could lose some business."

Salesperson (ramification question): "And possibly some customers?"

Prospect: "Possibly."

Salesperson (ramification question): "What does this amount to in lost profits?"

Prospect (beginning to see need): "I never figured it out, but it probably could run into tens of thousands of dollars."

Note: Perhaps for the first time, the prospect has focused on the consequences of the situation: tens of thousands of dollars in lost profits.

Salesperson (payoff question): "If I could show you a way to get those messages to all your branches simultaneously so that you can prevent lost sales and customers, would that be of interest?"

Prospect: "I'd be interested in knowing what you have."

Note: The salesperson *intensified* the need by getting the prospect to recognize the real effect of late messages—a loss of profits. He projected the negative consequences of the situation then followed up with a payoff question to suggest a solution and whet the prospect's appetite to hear it. "If I could show you a way to get those messages to all your branches simultaneously so that you can prevent lost sales and customers, would that be of interest?"

The prospect asks for the solution by responding, "I'd be interested in knowing what you have."

At this point, if the salesperson has not already qualified the prospect as to investment decision authority, he will do it now. Before making his presentation or demonstration, he will settle the price issue and when the prospect would want to begin the installation if he was convinced the solution would work.

The presentation will simply be the proof and demonstration of how the problem will be solved. *The sale is virtually closed during the questioning process.*

Note: Many sales are actually closed in the questioning process. The presentation, proposal, or demonstration are just formalities.

Why ask a ramification question if you already know what the ramifications are?

It is much more effective to have the prospect discover the problem for himself. When you tell him what the consequences or ramifications of the situation are, he may see this as self-serving and be less likely to agree. When he discovers it for himself, he is actually selling himself. It is the "ah-hah" experience, self-discovery, at work. Of course, if the prospect does not acknowledge the consequences after your ramification questions, then you must suggest them and get agreement.

It is obvious that ramification questions intensify problems or opportunities. They help a prospect see the negative effects of the present situation or the opportunities for improvement. This makes the need *definite* and builds an urgency to act.

If ramification questions are so important, why do salespeople hesitate to use them?

1. Salespeople have been conditioned to be "tellers" rather than "askers." We are anxious to tell the prospect that he has a problem.

2. Salespeople assume that because a prospect acknowledges a problem exists, he views it as important. In fact, the prospect may have never considered it a problem before and may not consider it important enough to take action at this time. As mentioned before, we get accustomed to our problems and learn to live with them. Sometimes, we need to be "jolted" out of our complacency.

3. The salesperson may be afraid of offending a prospect by bringing up inadequacies or problems. However, most prospects will not be offended as long as you are asking, not telling.

4. And finally, the salesperson may be unaware of the ramifications of the problem because he really doesn't know what is going on in the prospect's operation. This requires application or industry knowledge and preparation. Thinking about the ramifications of the situation you are attempting to improve beforehand will enable you to prepare good ramification questions.

Probability of a Sale

1. When a salesperson makes a presentation based on uncovering indefinite needs, he has a low probability of a sale.

   Reason: The prospect does not see a clear need or fully understand the consequences of the present situation.

2. When a salesperson makes a presentation after asking ramification questions and uncovering definite needs, but without awakening the prospect's desire for a solution based on expectancy of results (payoff questions), the probability of a sale is medium to good.

   Reason: While the prospect sees the need, he has not yet expressed an interest in hearing the solution and may not be aware of the positive effects.

3. When a salesperson asks payoff questions that build up the prospect's desire for the solution and then makes a presentation with benefits related to the definite needs, his chances for closing the sale are high.

   Reason: The prospect has been promised a solution to a problem that he wants to solve. He is interested in hearing the salesperson's proposal.

Conclusion

Don't be too anxious to make your presentation. Make sure you have set the stage correctly by:

I. Qualifying the Prospect
   1. Identifying the decision makers
   2. Establishing a definite need
   3. Verifying the ability to pay
   4. Setting a decision time-frame
   5. Evaluating competitive bids
   6. Ensuring against hidden factors

II. Identifying Needs
   1. Asking fact-finding questions to uncover needs and dissatisfactions
   2. Asking problem-building questions to explore needs and dissatisfactions

III. Needs Intensification
   1. Asking ramification questions to reveal negative consequences of present situation and get the prospect to clearly see his need
   2. Asking payoff questions to promise a solution to problems and whet the prospect's appetite to hear your solution

The presentation is the culmination of the questioning process. This is where you present your solutions to the problems uncovered through questioning.

By the time you make a presentation or demonstration, your prospect should be at least 90 percent sold.

Remember: Sellin' ain't tellin'—it's askin'. Isn't it?

8
Making Presentations That Win

Sometimes I have nightmares. They have a consistent theme. I see myself walking into my doctor's office. You see, I've been a bad boy and ate all those delicious rich foods, drank too many high-calorie cocktails, and indulged excessively in creamy delights.

I'm sure that hasn't exactly done wonders for my cholesterol level. I'm concerned and go to have it checked.

Before I can say anything, the doctor greets me with a warm smile, rushes me into a chair, pulls out a flipchart and while turning brightly illustrated, preprinted pages, he exclaims enthusiastically:

> *Arnie, I want to tell you about our special for the month. We're offering a 20 percent discount on appendectomies if we can get you under the knife by the 31st—and if you can find a friend, there's an additional 10 percent discount for the second patient. We're also featuring a half-price sale on hemorrhoid treatments—a very good buy if I may say. And oh yes, our super special is on ulcerated colitis. Go in within ten days and save 33-1/3 percent. How does that sound, Arnie, can we sign you up?*

After awakening from this bizarre dream, I begin to fathom it's real meaning.

Ye Gad! It's me making a presentation to a prospect. No questions, no listening, no qualification, no uncovering a need. I'm like a doctor offering a diagnosis before examining the patient to find out what's wrong with him—if anything. I'm just spouting off what I've got to sell— hoping it will ring a bell.

The nightmare is true!

News Flash: Tens of millions of drill bits were sold last year to buyers who didn't really want to buy drill bits. What they wanted was *holes.*

News Flash: A leading manufacturer of lawn mowers displayed colorful pictures of the company's product in national magazines. The company was advised by it's marketing consultants that potential buyers were not really interested in lawn mowers. They were interested in beautifully cut, manicured lawns. As a result, the company began to feature the end result benefit—"pictures of beautifully cut, manicured lawns"—instead of the feature—the lawn mower—in their national advertising.

News Flash: Here is what would-be buyers of glass-enclosed sun rooms were promised in a direct mail letter:
   "An elegant and gracious living area in your home."
   "An indoor garden atmosphere of serenity, beauty, and comfort."
   "Complete relaxation, better health, and enjoyment."

What is the message contained in the examples above? People buy benefits, therefore sell benefits—benefits—benefits!

The idea that buyers buy benefits, not features, is far from new. Most salespeople learn about selling benefits early in their careers.

However, despite knowing what to do "intellectually," many salespeople still fail to convert features into benefits meaningful to the buyer. They assume that prospects will translate "obvious" features into benefits on their own. In addition, they often fail to state the benefit so it has the maximum impact on the potential user.

Let's define features and benefits. A feature is a prominent part, characteristic, structure, or form of a product or service. It describes what the product is, how it is made, or how it works. It is a *fact*.

For example, "This camera comes equipped with a built-in self-timer." This is a feature. It describes a characteristic of the product, a fact.

A benefit describes how a feature of a service or product satisfies, helps, or is advantageous to the person using it. It tells what the feature does for the users (how they gain or benefit from it).

In the example above, the built-in self-timer was the feature. Now for the same example, a salesperson would point out the benefit in this way, "Now you can get into your own pictures without having someone take them. This adds *convenience* and *more fun* to taking pictures with this camera." The benefit words are *underlined*. The prospect is buying convenience and fun, not a built-in self-timer.

Let's add one more term to the feature benefit glossary, "related benefit." A related benefit is a benefit applied to the specific, definite need(s) of the individual you are selling. It tells how a product feature meets a personal need expressed by that person.

In the following example, note how the salesperson personalizes the benefits of compact size and lightweight to the prospect.

"Mrs. Harris, I know that you and Mr. Harris travel a lot, and that size and weight are important to you. Look how compact and lightweight this camera is, yet sturdy and durable to withstand heavy use. Isn't this the ideal camera for your upcoming trip to the Far East?"

Prospects buy related benefits because related benefits answer the WIIFM (What's in it for me?) question that every prospect asks whether expressed or unexpressed.

The "So What" Test for Benefits

When converting a feature into a benefit, one way to make sure that the benefit is personally meaningful to the customer is to ask yourself "So what" after each benefit statement.

Salesperson: "These equipment stands are made from galvanized aluminum."

Prospect: "So What?"

Salesperson: "They won't rust."

Prospect: "Nice—but so what?"

Salesperson: "What this means to *you*, Mr. Prospect, is that you will reduce your annual replacement cost by 40 percent."

Prospect: "Oh—that's interesting!"

Connecting Features and Benefits

Don't assume that your prospect will automatically convert the feature into a benefit. That's your job.

Your prospect is not necessarily thinking in this way at the time you make your presentation and might miss the real benefits of your product or service unless you clearly state them. Make a habit of translating every feature into a benefit by means of a "bridging" word or phrase such as "which means" or "thus". Here is an example. "We provide professional investment management for the individual investor, based on our thirty years of experience."

This is a feature statement describing what the company does and how long it has been in business. Interesting, but "so what."

By using the phrase "this means," we convert the feature into a benefit and then relate the benefit to the prospect's individual needs:

"*This means*, Mr. Prospect, you can anticipate *above market returns* on your investment with the *security* and *peace of mind* that your investment will be *protected* in a down market. You can do what you do best, Mr. Prospect, which is to *run your business profitably*, while we do what we do best, *make your money earn more money for you.*"

Take your benefit out to its maximum impact. This may even require stating the benefit of a benefit.

A final point about features and benefits. Just because competition offers the same or similar features is not a reason for you to leave them out of your presentation. If you don't mention them, the prospect may assume you don't have them.

Organizing and Delivering the "Winning" Presentation

Lets examine the steps in making a winning presentation.

Step 1: *Set a presentation objective.*

To give direction to your presentation, you should be very clear on what your presentation, demonstration, or proposal is designed to accomplish. Is it ease of operation, price, speed, economy, durability, ability to handle multiple jobs, peace of mind, or perhaps a combination of several factors?

Ask yourself this question: "What do I need to persuade my prospect of in order for him to take the action that I want him to take?"

Your presentation objective needs to be:

1. Directive—State specifically what your presentation is designed to prove.
2. Prospect oriented—Tell how your prospect will benefit.
3. Realistic—State the realistic action you can expect your prospect to take as a result of your presentation.

Here is an example of a copier salesperson's objective in making a demonstration to a large potential user:

"If I can persuade Superior Financial, Ltd., that the automatic feeding and sorting capability of the Wizard A 1-0 copier (directive) can save clerical time and reduce errors (prospect oriented), then they'll order two machines for a pilot test *now* and fifty more following the test (realistic)."

Know what your presentation is designed to accomplish in specific terms. If you did a good job of questioning, you will have established your prospect's definite needs.

Step 2: *Study your audience.*

What perspectives, attitudes, knowledge, or biases does your audience bring to the presentation?

If the financial person is present, he may be evaluating your presentation in terms of budget constraints, cash requirements, or leasing versus buying The operations person may have concerns such as quality control, employee training, operating efficiency, and maintenance.

Know who will be present and what they are looking for. Be prepared to address their concerns. Of course, if there is a large group, you can't be all things to all people, but know who the key players are and understand their viewpoints.

Determine whether your primary audience is made up of feelers, thinkers, intuitors, or sensors. Where possible, plan to use words and techniques that will make your presentation more acceptable to the key person you are communicating with. Remember that thinkers prefer factual presentations, sensors are bottom-line oriented, feelers relate to a personal approach, and intuitors look for innovation and creativity.

The presentation itself is not the time to get your prospects to do a 180 degree turn. Your audience should be predisposed to your offering *before* the actual presentation. Arrange private meetings with key individuals, provide print material for those you *can't meet* with beforehand so they are briefed, put on minipresentations before the "main event," and have your technical people make a presentation (under your guidance) to the prospect's "techies." These activities get the audience on your side before the presentation.

You want to go into the presentation with the odds as much in your favor as possible. Make certain that the people in the prospect organization who are on your side are present at the meeting. Check out factors such as room size and decor, lighting, ventilation, refreshments, materials, audiovisuals, and possible distractions. Don't make your presentation just before lunch (your audience may be salivating—but not about your presentation), after a large lunch (especially an alcoholic one), or when your audience has just been through a traumatic experience (such as the loss of a large account or key employee).

Be in control by knowing your audience and having them predisposed to your offering.

Step 3: *Prepare a benefits information statement.*
What information should you include in your presentation?

To answer this question, ask yourself, "What benefits does my audience need to realize for them to take the action I want them to take? Rather than sift through a mass of data about your product, work from an audience perspective and provide only the information your audience needs to make an informed, positive decision.

Deciding what to leave out of a presentation is just as important as what information to include. We have so much information at our finger tips today that we suffer from "information overload" and "analysis paralysis." Using our copier example, the benefits we have come up with for our benefits information statement are:

- Operator training will be simplified.
- The price is competitive.
- Sorting time will be reduced.
- There will be fewer errors in collating.
- Operator time will be saved.
- The machine is relatively trouble free with minimal downtime.
- We provide fast, efficient service.
- There will be a reduction in filing space.

List the benefits in the order they come to mind. Under each benefit, list the sources of the benefit. The sources are the "features" or "facts" that support the benefit. In effect, these are the "proofs" that the benefit will be realized.

For example, under the benefit "sorting time will be reduced," the proof would be "a 20 bin sorter provides automatic sorting vs. present manual sorting."

Repeat this process for each benefit by listing the benefit and then the features or sources that support the benefit. Review your benefit information statement to make sure that the benefits relate to the prospect's *definite needs* and that the sources support the benefit they are listed under. You now have an outline of the information you need to include in your presentation.

Step 4: *Organize your benefits information statement.*
Which benefit should you present first? Is there a way to organize your information?

The answer is yes, there is a correct way, and it is to present your most powerful benefit (the one that is most important to your prospect) *first*. To grab your audience's attention and heighten interest, you want to lead off with your most compelling reason.

If you start off with lesser benefits, you may lose your audience and never get the chance to get to the meat of your presentation. Have you ever had the experience where the key person or persons had to leave unexpectedly after a short time? Besides, your number one benefit may be all that is required to close the deal. Don't present more than is necessary to reach your objective.

Arrange your benefit information statement (see Figure 8-1) with your most important benefit first. Place the other benefits in declining order of importance. Under each benefit, arrange your proofs in the same declining order of importance as the benefitts. You now have your information organized and you are ready to develop your actual presentation. Your benefits information statement is actually the agenda for your presentation. Figure 8-1 shows an example of a completed benefits information statement, organized in descending order of importance.

Figure 8-1
Benefits Information Statement
(Wizard A1-0)

Benefit 1: Reduce sorting time by 30%.
　　Features/Proofs — Present results of test comparing manual vs.
　　　　machine sorting

　　　　　　Test A: May 5, 19-- (750 documents)
　　　　　　Test B: May 6, 19-- (1075 documents)

　　　　— Demonstrate machine sorting features

Benefit 2: Reduce clerical document feeding time by 20%.
　　Features/Proofs — Present results of test comparing manual vs.
　　　　automatic feeding

　　　　　　Test C: May 6, 19-- (350 documents)

　　　　— Demonstrate automatic document feeder

Benefit 3: Reduce collating errors by 10%.
　　Features/Proofs — Present results of test comparing manual vs.
　　　　machine sorting

　　　　　　Test D: May 6, 19-- (1075 documents)

Benefit 4: Simplify operator training.
　　Features/Proofs — Demonstrate microcomputer controls
　　　　　　　— Demonstrate self-diagnostic codes

Benefit 5: Reduce downtime.
　　Features/Proofs — Present statistics from service records of
　　　　existing installations
　　　　　　　— Present testimonial letters from users

Benefit 6: Competitive pricing.
　　Features/Proofs — Present price list comparison with compet-
　　　　itive equipment
　　　　　　　— Present service contracts and warranty com-
　　　　parison with competitive vendors

You are now ready to begin writing your presentation.

Step 5. *Write the opening of your presentation*
Presentations may be one on one across the prospect's desk or a more formal, stand-up type before a group of people. Each requires a different approach, but the elements of the presentations are similar. A more formalized group presentation is described here, but you will be able to relate the basic structure to any kind of presentation you give, including written proposals.

The opening has five parts:
1. Build rapport.
2. State the problem or opportunity.
3. Present your credentials.
4. Outline the agenda.
5. Describe the action your audience is to take.

1. Build rapport. If you know your audience well, this may take the form of friendly greetings and references to a prior meeting or conversation.

If much of the audience is new to you, meeting them informally before the presentation is useful and will help you relax. When starting, make sure you have everyone's attention. Pause to let the chatter die down. Make a few brief remarks to lighten the situation such as expressing your appreciation for the presentation opportunity, a relevant story, a joke, or humorous anecdote.

Being well groomed, having a pleasant demeanor, knowing the names of the people in attendance, and being informed on your subject are all part of building rapport. Don't forget to smile. The purpose of this step is to build a bond with your audience. It is a good idea to have the members print their names boldly on tent cards with marking pens so you can refer to them by name during your presentation.

Here is an example of a rapport-building opening:
"Ladies and gentlemen, thank you for the opportunity to present the copier industry's standard of excellence, the Wizard A1-0. I appreciate your taking the time to visit our facility and attend this demonstration."

"I'd also like to thank Don Harris of your organization for his help in providing the information on your copying requirements and in conducting the tests comparing your present method with the proposed system."

2. State the problem or opportunity. In this part of the opening, you answer the question for your audience, "Why are we here? What is the problem or opportunity your presentation will address?" That is what your audience is interested in. Give them clear evidence that you understand their problem and that you are on their wavelength.

"With the increase in your sorting and collating requirements (coupled with severe demands on everyone's time due to reduced staff), your present machines are not equipped to handle your needs. You require state-of-the-art technology to meet your productivity goals."

3. Present your credentials. What are your personal or your organization's qualifications to solve this problem? Tell them of your experience in solving similar problems. Be specific. Use references and testimonials. Your credentials establish you as qualified to address their problem and demand their attention.

"Our company, Top of the World Copy Corporation, has installed over five thousand Wizard A1-0 units in financial institutions such as yours with excellent results."

4. Outline the agenda.
State your solution to their problem in the form of an agenda. These are the reasons they should buy. Your agenda is the list of benefits from your benefits information statement (which are in declining order of importance). Do not cover the proofs at this time.

By presenting an agenda, you are actually giving your audience a road map, a menu, the sequence your presentation will take and what it will cover.

Here is an example of an agenda being presented:
"What you will be seeing today is how the Wizard A1-0 copier, truly a modern miracle, will enable Superior Financial to:
• Reduce sorting time by 30%.
• Reduce document feeding time by 20%.
• Reduce collating errors by 10%.
• Simplify and speed up operator training.
• Reduce downtime.
"You will be able to do all of these things with an investment in equipment that is competitively priced to any comparable model on the market."

Your audience now knows what you will be presenting and in which order. You may want to have your agenda on a visual such as a flip chart or overhead.

5. Describe the action your audience is to take. Here you inform your audience of what action they will be expected to take as a result of your presentation. You are, in effect, asking for the order up front.

"At the conclusion of this demonstration, I believe you will be convinced that our Wizard A1-0 copier is the ideal copier for your specific needs.

"We will ask for your agreement to an initial order of two machines for a pilot test to be followed by fifty more after three months."

Your presentation should be interactive. Get your audience involved right from the beginning. After stating the problem you might ask for agreement. "Bill, is that your understanding of the problem?" "Gene, do you want to add anything?"

Before you move into the body of your presentation, make sure everyone is "on board" and comfortable with the agenda and action step.

The introduction can be short, but it sets the tone for the entire presentation. Practice your introduction so that it is directive, enthusiastic, rapport building, and "hooks" your audience right from the start. If your introduction is done smoothly and confidently, the likelihood is that the rest of the presentation will also flow nicely. It is a good idea to memorize the opening so that you'll build confidence in your ability to get off to a good start.

Step 6: *Write the body of your presentation.*
In the body, you present each of the benefits in declining order of importance.

The process is as follows:
1. Present the first benefit (the most important one).
2. Tell how you will deliver the benefit.
3. Present the "proofs" that support the benefit. Proofs can be in the form of:
   • A demonstration
   • Fact sheets
   • An independent study

- Third-party testimonials
- A test or comparison

4. Solicit questions and get agreement (trial close).
5. Restate the benefit.
6. Proceed to the next benefit.

Each benefit you present is actually a minipresentation in which you introduce the benefit, describe it, get agreement, and summarize.

Make the presentation a *dialogue* as opposed to a *monologue*. Encourage the audience to ask questions. "Is it clear to you, Phil, how we arrived at the 30 percent savings in sorting time?" Use trial closes to get agreement. "Isn't the forty copies per minute speed of this unit impressive?" Don't move on to the next benefit until you have gained your audience's concurrence. If you receive strong buying reactions, consider going right to the close at this point.

Repeat the above process for each benefit listed on your benefits information statement. By dealing with one benefit at a time, it is easier for your audience to follow your presentation. Cover only as many benefits as you need to get the desired action. Your prospect's reactions, verbal and physical, will often signal you when to close. We will cover closing in more detail in chapter ten. After you've presented the body, you are now ready for the close.

Step 7. *Write the close of your presentation.*

You have presented the benefits and feature proofs from your benefits information statement. Questions have been raised and you have handled them. Now it is time for a firm, motivating call for action. Summarize by stating the original problem.

"Bill, your present system lacks the automatic sorting and document-feeding capability that you urgently require."

Now give a shortened presentation of your benefit information statement.

"We've shown you that our equipment can reduce sorting time, reduce document feeding time, and simplify operator training, and it's evident our equipment is durable and dependable." (Now CLOSE!)

"I'd like to get your order today for two machines, which we can deliver within thirty days so we can start your test."

You may have noticed that the format for the *opening, body,* and *close* of your presentation could be described as:

1. "Tell 'em what you're going to tell 'em" (opening).
2. "Tell 'em" (body).
3. "Tell 'em what you've told 'em" (close).

This builds repetition and reinforcement into your presentation, important factors in gaining acceptance of your ideas.

Step 8. *Decide on language.*

When making a presentation, the words you use and how you say them are important. Here are some pointers:

Speak naturally. Don't assume the role of an orator, performer, or evangelist. You are a presenter, the humble servant of your audience. Be yourself. Let your personality come through. Your prospect is buying *you* as well as your offering.

Use the active voice. This means putting the subject before the verb as in "this system is flexible" as opposed to "flexibility can be realized with this system" or "we'll take action" instead of "action will be taken by us."

Use personalized language. Say "our system" and "your operation" instead of the more impersonal "the" or "it." Use people's names and the name of the company such as "Superior Corp will benefit" as opposed to "the company will benefit."

Be concrete and specific. "We've been in business for fourteen years" sounds better than "We've been in business for a long time" or "We have more than one thousand customers" as opposed to "We have a large number of customers."

Use short sentences and short words. Our natural mode of conversation is to use shorter sentences and simpler words than when we write. Do it in your presentation and you will sound more natural. It is a myth that big words will impress others. The goal is to get your message across so you are understood.

Use jargon carefully. To people unfamiliar with your field, jargon can be distracting and offensive. Use it judiciously.

Avoid cliches and overworkeed words. Try to avoid the above by expressing your thoughts in your own words. Do some of these words sound overused?

"The greatest"

"Fantastic"

"High-tech"

"State of the Art"
"Interface"
"Viable"
A good test for your language is your own ear. Do you sound natural and relaxed or do you sound like a memo?

Step 9. *Select audiovisuals.*
Visuals enhance a presentation. The more of your audience's senses you can bring into play, the greater the impact of your message.

When you speak, you affect your audience's auditory sense. Visuals such as a portfolio, flip chart, slides, overheads, or video engage the visual sense and create dual sensory perception (hearing and seeing). A demonstration where the prospect touches the machine, smells the fragrance, tastes the wine, or feels the material affects the kinesthetic senses, the senses of feel, touch, taste, and smell. A good presentation will attempt to engage as many of the senses as possible.

Factors such as room temperature, lighting, ambience, background noise, and competing stimuli such as telephone calls, unannounced visitors, and outside noise affects the outcome of your presentation. You are not always in a position to control these factors, but if you have an important presentation, make an effort to ensure that your audience is comfortable, that you have the proper audiovisual equipment, and that there are no distractions or interruptions. Stand in the back of the room and on the extreme sides to make sure your audience can see and hear satisfactorily from any area in the room.

Your audiovisuals should enhance your presentation, not dominate it. They should give emphasis and clarity to your key points. Slides and overheads should be simple, clear, attractive, and uncluttered. A flip chart neatly prepared can be very effective in allowing the audience to follow your key points.

Handouts that are concise and support the main theme and that do not distract your audience from your presentation are good tools.

Overheads, slides, audio, and video presentations require more preparation but, if done professionally, can add a significant dimension to your message.

Audiovisuals should enable your audience to more easily understand your presentation and make it more interesting and exciting. They should not be used to impress people with your creativity and distract from the message.

In choosing presentation materials, use the method that your prospect is most accustomed to and comfortable with. If he prefers to have presentations done visually, accommodate him. Personalize your materials as much as possible and use examples and illustrations that relate to the prospect's business.

Preparing Written Proposals

The steps in preparing a written proposal are similar to those used to prepare an oral presentation. Proposals have an opening, body, and close. Review the presentation steps when you write your next proposal. Make sure your proposal states the objective and the benefits to be gained. If your proposal is lengthy, use a table of contents.

A word of caution: don't write a proposal unless you have to. When a prospect asks for a proposal, find out what he means by "proposal." Some people simply want the "prices" in writing. Others use it as a stall to defer making a decision.

Before you spend hours of your valuable time as well as your secretary or typist's time, be sure that a proposal is really necessary and determine what it needs to contain.

Where possible, proposals should be delivered in person and presented by you to the person or persons who are getting the proposal. Give each individual a copy and read the proposal aloud while they follow along. Stop at key points along the way to elaborate or answer questions. The proposal then becomes a presentation—you can now make the words come to life.

If the proposal is involved and contains technical data, cover the sections that can be read verbatim and summarize the other sections.

Get agreement and understanding as you go along.

You may opt to leave out the "investment" page until you have completed reviewing the proposal. Then hand out the investment page and cover it. Some prospects will go directly to the investment page when you hand them the proposal and will focus on the price before you have had a chance to justify it.

On the other hand, you may want to discuss the investment first to clear the air and give your prospect the opportunity to weigh the ensuing benefits against the required investment. This is a judgment call and depends on the situation.

Let's Summarize

1. Write out the *objective* of your presentation, demonstration, or proposal so that it clearly states what you need to persuade your prospect of, what benefits he will get, and what action you can realistically expect.
2. Study your audience. Gear your presentation to the perspectives, attitudes, and knowledge of the key players.
3. Decide on the information you are going to present by writing out a benefits information statement.
4. Organize the information in descending order of importance—importance to your audience, that is.
5. Design a strong opening.
6. Prove the benefits in the body.
7. Close convincingly.
8. Think about the words you will use and rehearse.
9. Use appropriate visual aids.
   And finally,
10. Practice, practice, practice.

The best way to become a good presenter is to make lots of presentations. You will gain confidence, benefit by your mistakes, and ultimately come to really enjoy the challenge of persuading others to your point of view.

9
Objections, Objections, and Still More Objections

Your price is too high!

It's not the right color.

You caught me at a bad time.

It's very noisy.

Too complicated. Our people couldn't handle it.

We can't take a chance on something that new.

Objections weigh me down. Some of them are so banal, I get angry. Who said the 'customer is always right?' I don't know if they mean what they say or if they're just excuses. God, give me strength.

Objections—negative, unfavorable, or cynical reactions to the salesperson's claims and assertions. Feelings or expressions of doubt, opposition, distaste, or disapproval.

No matter how much trust building you do or how well you are prepared, it is a certainty that you will get some resistance.

Some of the reasons can be attributed to buying psychology and are out of the salesperson's control. Customers do not want to appear too easy. They feel the tougher they are, the sharper your pencil gets. Some want to test how much you really know or how badly you want the business. Objections may be a manifestation of aversion to change or fear of making decision. They may mask a distrust or dislike of you, the salesperson, or your company. Your prospects may feel a loyalty to their present representatives who saw them through tough times or an emotional attachment to products or organizations that have given them good service over the years. Your competitor may have prompted prospects to ask questions that he hopes will put you on the defensive.

Let's face it, salespeople, like politicians, are not perceived as the most forthright people, and buyers have been conditioned to accept what we say with a grain of salt. It is natural for them to express skepticism no matter how truthful you are in what you say.

However, we as salespeople are not without blame in causing prospects to raise objections. Here are some of the things we do (or don't do) that cause our prospects to raise objections.

1. We fail to establish trust and rapport up-front and maintain it throughout the entire sales process. Keep in mind that prospects' emotional or psychological needs as well as their logic needs must be satisfied continuously.

2. We are not always clear on how our product or service will benefit the prospect. We sometimes:
- Assume prospects are more knowledgeable than they are, and we don't take the time to ensure that we have explained ourselves clearly and that our prospects understand.
- Use industry buzz words, abstract terms, technical language, or jargon with prospects who are not familiar with them.
- Fail to use "bridges" or connecting words or statements that tie ideas together in a logical flow or to relate product features to the benefits they produce.
- Fail to use visuals, testimonials, and other aids and proof sources that enhance understanding and credibility.

3. We present the wrong benefits. A benefit statement to one person may be an objection to another. A typewriter salesperson who emphasizes that the typist will turn out "more work" with his new machine may appeal to the boss but could "turn off" the operator. She will react more favorably to such benefits as ease of operation, quietness, fewer errors, less fatigue, and a pleasing design and appearance. Benefits should relate to the prospect's personal and emotional as well as logical needs.

4. We talk to the wrong person, one who does not have the authority to buy, who is not personally affected by our solution to the problem, or who is not willing to take a "risk," leading to objections.

5. We fail to get agreement early in the interview and making sure the prospect is "in step" with us during the selling cycle. Some prospects tune you out early on but don't let you know until you are through with your presentation. Trial closes or verifying questions or statements will ensure that your prospect understands and accepts your stated points throughout your presentation.

For example, "Mr. Johnson, does our two minute transmitting and receiving speed meet your requirements?" or "Can you see how the new 8mm format will reduce your mailing costs?"

6. We use examples, illustrations, or "war stories" that do not apply to the prospect. Telling a small businessman that General Motors has used your product successfully may give him the wrong message— that you are really geared to handling big business. Your prospect is the center of his own universe. Get into **his** world, work from his sense of reality.

7. We fail to get on the same "communicating channel" as the prospect. If you're dealing with a primary sensor, use a stripped-down, botton-line approach. Thinkers want facts, alternatives, and logic. Feelers want to sense that you have a personal interest in them, and intuitors are interested in how your offering fits into the big picture.

8. We fail to display confidence and a belief in our ability to deliver satisfaction to the prospects. If they sense that you lack commitment, knowledge, and enthusiasm or that you are more interested in making the sale than in solving their problems, it will raise doubts that they will get what they are looking for, and those doubts will be translated into buying resistance.

Your Attitude Toward Objections

If you accept objections as a normal step in the selling process, a step that you can and will handle in a positive manner, then you will maintain the right attitude and not be defeated by objections.

Remember, an objection is **not** a rejection. Repeat, an objection is **not** a rejection.

In making a purchase, how many times have you raised one or more objections and still bought after the salesperson satisfied your concerns? You wanted to be convinced that you were making the right choice. Objections can be positive.

I think we'll agree that the toughest customer to sell is the one that offers no feedback. At least an expressed objection enables us to know where the prospect stands. In some cases, the objection may really be a question, a request for more information or to clarify an issue that the prospect is fuzzy on.

In fact, in most cases, if you are well prepared and know your prospect's needs, you will be in a stronger selling position after you have handled the objection than before.

Objections can occur at any point in the selling process. The following are some simple rules for keeping objections in the right perspective.

1. Make sure you understand the objection. Listen carefully. There is a difference between a question and an objection. One asks for information, the other expresses an attitude. Don't respond immediately. Take your time. Get clarification if necessary. Salespeople are so accustomed to hearing the same objections that even the mere allusion to it sets off an automatic reaction.

One way to ensure that you understand the objection is to get the prospect to be more specific. For example, your prospect makes the statement, "Why have we had **so many** breakdowns on your Gismatic?" Before answering the objection, you might ask, "Mr. Prospect, when you say 'so many,' exactly what do you mean? Or, "Mr. Prospect, how do you define a breakdown?"

For one prospect, "so many" might mean once a month; for another, once a week, and for yet another, once every three months. Another prospect might regard a "breakdown" as running out of supplies or a power shortage affecting the entire building.

You need to clarify these abstract responses to know what you're dealing with. You may be surprised to learn that the nature of the problem is a lot different than you suspected and that the objection expressed is only a surface remark.

2. Make it OK for your prospect to raise the objection. Try to see the prospects' concern from their viewpoints. Don't argue. Don't panic.

Let them know that you can understand why they might feel that way. If you were in their shoes, you might feel the same way. Objections thrive on opposition, but die with agreement.

3. Decide whether the objection is valid or invalid. Valid objections are those that are raised because of a perceived limitation or short-coming of your product or service. An invalid objection is a put-off, excuse, stall, or smokescreen. It often hides the real objection or indicates a disinterest on the part of the prospect.

Valid objections should be accepted at face value and answered directly. Invalid objections, such as "we're too busy right now" or "there's no money in the budget" are handled differently and will be covered shortly.

A price objection raised early in the selling interview is often invalid. If price is brought up after you have had a chance to present the benefits, it is likely to be valid and needs to be answered.

4. Prepare yourself and your presentation to anticipate the most common objections. This is where pre-call planning can help. This will give you confidence, and you will not easily be thrown off track. Role-play anticipated objections with a colleague or into an audio-cassette player and listen to how you sound. If you are sure an objection will be raised, bring it up yourself. This takes the edge off and makes the objection less important to the prospect. However, be careful not to raise objections that the prospect has not considered—even though you are confident you have the answer.

5. View objections as proof that your prospect is interested in your offering. The most difficult prospects to sell are those that provide no feedback.

6. Adopt the attitude that by raising objections, your prospects are really seeking more information—that they want to be convinced that they are making the right decisions.

7. Develop the right "mental set" for objections. Objections are not rejections. It is not your worth as a person that is being threatened, it is your role as a salesperson. Objections are generally directed at ideas, products, services, and policies. If you let the objection affect your self-image, your identity as a person, you will not be able to maintain the objectivity and mental toughness so vital to success in selling. This is easier said than done, but if you use the affirmation "I can't control the way I feel" (disappointed, defensive, tense), but I can control the way I think and act (positive, purposeful, and professional)" it will help you get through the difficult times.

There is a sale made on every sales call. Either the salesperson "sells" the prospect that the benefits of his prodeuct outweigh the price, or the prospect "sells" the salesperson that he doesn't need it, can't afford it, or it's not the right time.

The sales professional empathizes with prospects, but doesn't sympathize with or buy their excuses. He knows that if he doesn't make the sale, the prospects have lost more than the salesperson.

This attitude conveys the message, "You didn't buy, but I sincerely believe you should have bought because it was right for you." The prospect will remember this and may change his mind when the need arises again.

When you convince yourself that no single sale will have a monumental affect on your career or life, you will approach each situation with more confidence and positive expectancy and rid yourself of the fears of objections and of asking for the order. The best way to do this is to have a lot of prospects so that no single loss can make a severe impact.

Handling Invalid Objections

Invalid objections are excuses and put-offs and have no basis in fact. They arise usually because the prospect believes that there will be no benefit in talking to you and is disinterested. They are the knee-jerk reactions that many people have to salespeople. Most objections on the phone when you're prospecting for appointments are invalid. Examples are "You hit me at a bad time," "My partner is out of town," and "Money is tight." Here are some tactics you can use for invalid objections:

1. *Direct the dialogue to something you both can agree on.* "I can appreciate that money is tight, but if you can attract more people into the booth, you will increase sales and profits."

2. Delay your response. Prospect: "What will it cost me?" Salesperson: "Good question. I'll cover it shortly."

3. Give a token response and ask for more information. Prospect: "It's a good idea, but it won't work here." Salesperson: "Oh that's interesting. Why do you say that?"

4. Ignore the objection (selective listening). Use your good judgment on this one. Prospect: "You salespeople are all alike, thinking about your commissions." Salesperson: Says nothing. Continues on with his presentation.

5. Sometimes humor can defuse an objection.
A videotape salesperson got this objection from his prospect who was testing the tape. "Why are we experiencing all these dropouts?" The salesperson responded, "You're not getting **all** of them—my customer down the block is getting some of them, too."

If an invalid objection is mentioned more than once, treat it as a valid objection and respond immediately.

Valid objections are based on perceptions or information that the prospect has about your product or company. You will need to respond to these objections quickly and knowledgeably.

The Five Cs

The following is a five-step process for answering objections. We call it the five Cs process. Before we explain the five steps, let's examine how a prospect feels after he has raised an objection. Generally, he expects a rebuttal from the salesperson and has his defenses up. He is aware that he has challenged you, expects you to defend your position, and is prepared to defend his. When a person is in a defensive posture, indicative that he senses threat, he is not in the most logic-receptive frame of mind.

Therefore, the first step in the objection-handling process is to get the prospect off the defensive and into a receptive state.

Step 1: Clarify
Clarification is the process of ensuring that you and the prospect fully understand the objection. The technique for doing this is active

listening and reflection. We indicate to the prospect our genuine desire to understand his concerns by reflecting back to him in our own words both the feeling and content of what he has just stated. In this manner, we show the prospect that we not only understand him, but we accept his right to his point of view. We give him understanding and acceptance, two things people want from each other and that are crucial to good communications. Acceptance does not mean that we agree with his objection or point of view. What we accept is his right to his opinion, even though we don't necessarily agree with him. By giving the prospect the respect of hearing him out without rancor or retaliation, we establish trust and rapport and increase our chances of a fair hearing in return.

In active listening and reflection, we don't judge, evaluate, argue with, or question the prospect's logic. We simply restate or paraphrase what he said in a neutral manner to demonstrate understanding.

> Prospect objection: "I don't mind spending money, but I'm not about to waste it on overpriced, fancy equipment."

> Salesperson (using active listening and reflection):
> "Mr. Prospect, you seem annoyed because you think you are paying for more than you need. Is that a fair statement?"

> Prospect objection: "Your proposal looks OK, but we're not going to upset our whole system to find out."

> Salesperson (using active listening and reflection):
> "What I hear you saying is that you like our approach, but you're concerned about the installation?"

Note that the salesperson's response reflects both the feeling and the content that the prospect expressed and is not argumentative or judgmental. He simply lets the prospect know that, "I heard what you said and it's OK for you to say it."

The ball is in the prospect's court and he can do one of two things. First, he can acknowledge your understanding and expand his original statement. It also gives him an opportunity to vent his feelings—get it out of his system. In addition, it buys you some time to prepare your response. Second, he could let you know that you misunderstood his real objection and he will then clarify it.

In either case, you are ahead of the game and have a more relaxed prospect to deal with. It's hard for a prospect to disagree with a salesperson who understands and accepts his point of view.

Step 2: *Confirm*

When you have completed step one, clarification, you have uncovered the real objection. You get confirmation of this by turning the objection into a question—a question that you can answer. For example, "Mr. Prospect, your question is, will our MT 1300 editor stand up to a double-shift operation, is that correct?" Or, "As I understand it, Mr. Prospect, your real concern is in reducing phone costs enough to offset the increased monthly payments, right?"

You are ready to respond to an objection when you are sure in your own mind what you need to prove. I want to stress that it is important to get the prospect to be specific. Do not accept vague, general, abstract statements.

> Prospect: "We need a unit that's sturdy."
> Salesperson: "What do you mean by sturdy?"

> Prospect: "We're going to give your recommendations careful consideration."
> Salesperson: "Jack, when you say careful consideration, just what do you mean?"

> Prospect: "We always buy from the lowest bidder."
> Salesperson: "Always?"

> Prospect: "Most of our sales reps are experienced."
> Salesperson: "Most?" or "When you say **experienced**, what does that mean?"

Get concrete, quality responses. Specifics you can deal with. After you have clarified and confirmed an objection that appears to be the major stumbling block, you might ask, "Is there anything else standing in your way of making a 'go' decision?" If the answer is "no," you have a sale if you can answer the objection to the prospect's satisfaction. If he responds otherwise, you must fish out the real objection or realize you have a ways to go.

Step 3: Convince
This is the step where you answer the objection, marshaling all the facts and benefits at your command.

The convince step draws on your product knowledge, competitive knowledge, application knowledge, and knowledge of your customer's business and his emotional needs and wants. There's no faking it. You need to have the answers.

Usually, prospect objections to a product or service can be grouped into five or six categories. The rest are variations on the theme. List the most common objections and write out the best responses. Practice using these responses and refine them through personal experience. Create an objections handbook that contains all the possible objections you may get and the best responses.

Your belief in your product and company and your faith in your own ability is critical in how convincing you are. You must have the courage of your convictions and the courage to tell prospects things they may not want to hear.

Justifying a price for a quality product can be frustrating when the prospect is "strictly" a price buyer. Fortunately, there are not that many strictly price buyers around. Buyers do not want to spend money on features they perceive as window dressings, but they will buy quality. There are record sales of BMWs, Mercedes Benzs, Rolex watches, and Sony video equipment—all at higher prices than competitive products.

Selling value is one of the skills a sales professional must master. You stress quality, long-run economy, prestige, and durability to justify the price differential. This subject is treated more fully in chapter ten, The Psychology of Closing.

The objection stage is where salespeople show their true mettle. The sale begins when the customer says "no!"

References to satisfied users, testimonial letters, and impartial surveys are good evidence to introduce in the convince stage. The three Fs (feel, felt, found) work well here. For example, "Mr. Prospect, I understand how you **feel** about using a new product. Barbara Houghton over at Warnco **felt** the same way when she first started using our modems. Now she's **found** that she's getting better results than ever from her data network."

A word of caution. Provide just enough information to answer the objection. If someone asks you what time it is, don't tell him how to build a watch.

Step 4: Confirm

After you have answered the objection, confirm the fact that your prospect has accepted your response. Use a confirming question or statement such as, "So you see by this demonstration, the new Power-Tech terminal is easy to operate, fast, and can handle your long messages, don't you agree?" Or, "Do your feel more comfortable now, Mr. Lewis, knowing that the unit is not only lightweight but rugged as well?"

Step 5: Close

Once you've answered the objection and received confirmation of the prospect's acceptance, you must ask for action. This may consist of asking for an order, getting the go-ahead to continue with the presentation, or obtaining permission to see the decision maker. After you meet an important objection, view this as a form of prospect acceptance and request action.

"Mr. Manning, now that you see the applicability of this unit to your needs, when would you like delivery? I can have it for you on Friday."

To review, the five Cs are clarify, confirm, convince, confirm, and close.

The three Fs, which you may use in the convince stage, are feel, felt, and found.

One More Thought on the Price Objection

When price is a valid objection, it requires specific techniques. If you qualified your prospect and brought up the price issue early, you are less likely to have to deal with it later. It is better for prospects to have a general ideal of what the investment will be than to spring it on them at the end.

The price objection is covered in the next chapter, on closing, but one point needs to be brought out now. Don't misinterpret a buyer's, "Can you do better on the price?" ploy as a real objection. Smart buyers will raise the question figuring they have nothing to lose. Treat it as a strong buying signal. Smile and let the prospect know that he is getting the best price and that he has made a wise decision and a good buy. Write up the order. Regard it as an invalid objection and as a "nice try" by the prospect.

Handling objections requires good listening skills, a positive attitude, and excellent product and industry knowledge. Work on your active listening technique. It is amazing how much better at listening you will get when you have to reflect other people's feelings and content.

Build your objections handbook. Update it constantly so you have the best responses available to you in countering objections.

Remember that "objections thrive on opposition but die with agreement." Get on the same side as your prospect and attack the problem—not each other.

10
The Psychology
of Closing

*My first full-time job in selling was in the early 50s with
the Burroughs Adding Machine Company (later
Burroughs Corporation and now Unisys) in New York
City.*

*Our branch was a large one and the sales force was bro-
ken down into 'zones.' Each zone had a zone sales
manager with anywhere from five to ten sales
representatives reporting to him.*

*My first zone manager was Mort Klingon. Aside from
one or two experienced salespeople, Mort managed a
group of young 'tigers' like myself, eager but
inexperienced. Looking back, we were actually less like
'tigers' and more like 'bird dogs,' sniffing out the
prospects and bringing Mort in to close the deals. Mort
had a well-deserved reputation as a great 'closer,' and we
were all in awe of his ability to put the numbers up on
the board. He was smooth and effortless.*

*Oh, how I wished I could close like Mort. For a young,
inexperienced salesperson, just out of college, closing
held a mystique and special quality for me. I've gotten
better at it over the years, but asking the prospect to buy
still takes a conscious effort and creates uneasiness.*

Many salespeople today are reluctant to ask for the order. This is
understandable when you consider that after all the time and effort
salespeople have invested in their deals, the prospecting, rapport-

building, questioning, presentations, dealing with objections, and writing the proposal, the only justification for all this work is getting the order. No wonder there is so much emphasis put on the closing step and so much fear of getting a negative response.

The good "closers" in any sales organization have high esteem as well as high incomes.

It is interesting that when I ask the participants in my sales seminars the question, "How many of you regard yourself as a good closer," only 10 to 20 percent raise their hands.

Why is the percentage so low? Why does closing cause so much concern? Why do salespeople fear and avoid what should be a natural conclusion to the selling process but too often ends up in trauma, reducing them to timidity and indecision?

What is the single biggest reason salespeople don't ask for the order?

Fear of rejection!

They are worried that after all the work they have done, the prospect will say, "No."

It's that old ego getting in the way again. We have built up these nice relationships with our prospects, and now we have to ruin it all and ask them to buy. It would be much easier if the prospects would take the initiative and offer to buy.

Unfortunately, no matter how much they want what you are selling, prospects need to be gently "nudged" into buying. They expect the salesperson to ask for the business, and if you don't, they become skeptical about your belief in what you are selling and begin to doubt their own buying motives.

Have you ever been on the verge of a purchase only to get second thoughts when the salesperson let you off the hook by not asking for your order?

Prospects are not naive. They believe in the "hereafter"—they know what you're here after. Their own companies have salespeople, and they understand the salesperson's role.

They wouldn't be talking to you if they did not need or want your product. Of course, if you are focusing only on your own needs (your commission check for example), you cannot fully appreciate the value your prospect will derive from your product or service.

This is "win-lose" or high-pressure selling. If the sale is made, the salesperson "wins" and the prospect "loses."

If you have clearly identified your prospects' needs and feel confident that what you are selling meets those needs at a fair price, you have a "win-win" transaction. The prospects get what they want, you are paid for your efforts, and your company earns a legitimate profit. You should have no qualms about asking your prospects to take action if you truly believe it will help them. You will never be accused of being "pushy" or aggressive if you focus on the benefits the prospects will receive. It's when you are thinking about yourself and your needs that your attempts at closing are perceived as high pressure.

I believe the reason most salespeople don't regard themselves as good closers is because they don't know when to close. They set themselves up for rejection by not having correctly performed the steps leading up to the close.

You should not be asking for the order until you have a 90 percent (that's nine out of ten) or better chance of getting an affirmative response.

Asking for the order is not a "shot in the dark" or a manipulative maneuver that catches the prospect off-guard. It is rather the natural culmination of a progression of steps performed by the salesperson with his prospect during the selling process. By the time you reach the closing stage, the odds should be greatly in your favor. You will have recognized buying signals from the prospect, indicating that he has accepted your proposition and is ready to be closed.

Before we consider the techniques and attitudes necessary to be a good closer, here are two things you can do immediately to close more deals with less turmoil.

1. *To be a good closer, be a good opener.* Have a lot of prospects. Repeat. Have a lot of prospects.

If your closing ratio is one out of four prospects and you only have three prospects, you may go "0 for three."

If you have twelve prospects, even if you only close one out of six, you will get two orders. In addition, your mental outlook is much more positive when you have lots of deals going and this has an uncanny effect on prospects. The less you seem to need them, the more they want you.

When you only have a few deals, you start to press and call on your few prospects more than necessary. They sense this and tend to draw back, causing you to press even more.

Do a good job of prospecting and you will automatically become a better closer.

2. Close up front. Close your prospects right at the beginning. A good way to do this is to show them testimonial letters or refer to several satisfied customers with problems similar to theirs. Then say, "Mr. Prospect, my goal is to get a letter like this from you—and have you be glad to give it to me."

·In this way, you tactfully let your prospects know that you expect them to buy if you can meet their needs. But more importantly, you overcome your reticence to ask for the business by doing it in a natural and nonthreatening manner right at the beginning.

Let's review what has taken place before closing.

1. You identified the decision maker(s) or strong influencer(s) and involved them in the selling process. Each understands how they will "win" by supporting your proposal.

2. A definite need has been established and recognized by the prospect.

3. There is a budget for a specific amount available for funding the purchase.

4. You presented the benefits of your offering and related the benefits to the prospect's definite need(s).

5. You answered his questions and handled any objections raised by your prospect.

6. During the selling process, you established trust and rapport and gained agreement on key points through trial closes.

Rule 1 of Closing: Regard closing as a natural step in the selling process.

Having accomplished the above steps, it is only natural that you bring the process to a close by setting a delivery or installation date.

Rule 2 of Closing: Use trial closes, statements, or questions that gain your prospect's acceptance throughout the entire selling process.

A trial close is asking for the prospect's agreement on key points you have made during the sales interview. Trial closes help you verify your prospect's most important concerns and get his **acceptance** of one or more key points about your product or service.

Trial closes can be either nonthreatening questions or statements that:

A. Solicit additional information about the prospect's needs or desires.

B. Ask for his agreement to the WIIFM (what's in it for me) of a feature, benefit, or statement just made.

Trial closes are a way of taking the prospect's "buying temperature."

Professional salespeople continuously involve the prospect in the selling process and agreement through trial closes. Examples:

> "Mr. Prospect, does our eight-hour turnaround on color prints meet your rush requirements?"
>
> "It appears that getting 'Proof of Delivery' on your international shipments will give you the immediate assurance that you're looking for."
>
> "I think our new attractive gold line will appeal to your clientele, don't you?"
>
> "Does this approach to computerizing your inventory fit with your thinking?"

By asking for agreement early in the interview, you will have the time to deal with negative reactions, change your approach, or question for more information.

Many salespeople are so intent on "telling" their story, they don't take the time to find out if the prospect is buying in. Then, when it's too late, they learn that the prospect is not interested and time has run out.

Use trial closes:
- When presenting each major feature or benefit.
- After handling and overcoming an objection.
- Whenever you observe a buying signal.

Rule 3 of Closing: Watch your prospect like a hawk. Be alert for verbal and nonverbal buying signals and check them out with trial closes.

A buying signal is anything the prospect says or does that indicates he is favorably disposed to your proposition. Buying signals can be verbal or nonverbal.

Obvious verbal buying signals are statements such as:
- When can we get delivery?
- What colors does it come in?
- What are the terms?
- Who pays the freight?

Obvious nonverbal buying signals occur when:
- The prospect begins to study your literature or proposal more closely.
- The prospect suddenly relaxes from a formal posture.
- The prospect invites someone else in to listen to your story.

The following are some examples of buying signals. They may not be buying signals in every instance. Check them out. If you sense it is a buying signal, but you are not sure, use a trial close. A good one from noted sales trainer Lee Du Bois is, "Mr. Prospect, in your opinion, do you feel . . ." It is nonthreatening because it solicits the prospect's opinion and feeling instead of asking for a decision. Here's an example, "Mr. Prospect, in your opinion, do you feel that having your own private-label film would increase your profits?"

The prospect: Buying Signals

1. Picks up your proposal.
2. Says he might be interested in seeing a comparative survey.
3. Gives signs of wanting reassurance that he is making the right decision and is justified in acting now.
4. Cannot decide which of two products, colors, or quantities to select.
5. Assumes possession mentally. "Where's the best place to set up the unit?" "Who will do the training?"

6. Brings up the benefits of his present system or a competitive one so it can be compared to your proposal product or service.
7. Looks for a concession.
8. Opens or rubs his hands.
9. Makes gestures that involuntarily suggest he is almost ready (smiles or nods in agreement).
10. Has an increasingly friendly attitude toward you, your company, or your offering.
11. Rubs his chin thoughtfully.
12. Asks questions indicating specific area of interest.
13. Looks at your machine, literature, or proposal with increased interest.
14. Relaxes the muscles around his eyes and mouth.
15. Asks about final procedure. "What do I have to do to get started?"
16. Questions specific service or costs and starts calculating.
17. Expresses curiosity or interest by his reaction.
18. Asks others to sit in on the discussion or give their opinion.
19. Sits back in his chair and relaxes.
20. Leans forward so as to give maximum attention.
21. Suddenly holds all calls.
22. Begins to share confidential information.
23. Shows signs of excitement (speeds up talking or face lights up).

Not all buying signals are obvious. Many are of the nonverbal variety. I heard of an interesting one recently from one of our seminar participants. This president of an optical rep firm reported that one of his sales people knew it was time to close when a particular prospect began to hum. It seems that the salesperson hummed right along with the prospect as he wrote up the deal. (He claimed it was music to his ears.)

Can you think of one or two not-so-obvious verbal or nonverbal buying signals that you have observed that tipped you off that your prospect was really interested?

It is rare that prospects will come right out and tell you that they are ready to buy. However, they will tell you indirectly through verbal and nonverbal behavior. It is important that you pay close attention to your buyers' reactions during interviews.

Instead of focusing on yourself and what you are going to say, use a planned presentation that allows you the freedom to key on your prospects. Failure to be sensitive to prospects' reactions and to pick up on their buying signs can lead to unnecessary call backs or even lost sales.

Rule 4 of Closing: *The decision to buy is first made in the mind of the salesperson. The prospect need only agree with that decision.*

A closing question is any question whose answer confirms the fact that the prospect has bought. But who does the prospect confirm it to? He confirms it to himself.

By the time the salesperson asks a closing question, he already knows that the prospect has bought. The prospect, however, may not realize it. When you ask a closing question, you are helping the prospect to agree with a decision you have already made . . . that he has bought.

You know that he has mentally assumed possession by the statements and nonverbal behavior you have observed. All that is required now is that gentle nudge to overcome the buyer's natural inertia and make a final decision.

Rule 5 of Closing: *Learn several closing techniques that work in your business and have them ready at all times.*

Professional selling requires planning at virtually every step. Closing is no exception. You should have two or three prepared closes going into the sales call (pre-call planning). The mythical, quick-thinking, shoot-from-the-hip, extemporaneous salesperson will not last long in the selling arena with well-informed professional buyers. There are too many variables in the sales process, too many unexpected twists and turns in the road for you not to be as ready as you can be.

I am going to describe nine proven closing tactics plus some bonus ideas you can use to improve your closing average. Remember, these are techniques to move an interested prospect the final step and will not work unless the buyer is convinced of the benefits of your product.

You will need to adapt these methods to your own selling environment. Use the ones that are most applicable and comfortable for you.

In all of the closes, it is a good idea to summarize the major benefits before asking for the order. Although your prospect may be aware of the benefits, he may not bring them to mind at that moment unless you mention them.

Remember, a closing question is any question whose answer confirms the fact that the prospect has bought.

1. Assumptive Close. In the assumptive close, you assume that the prospect has bought and proceed to wrap up the deal. This method is sometimes call the "order book" close, because the salesperson takes out his order book or form and begins asking questions such as "What is the correct billing name," or "Where do you want it shipped?" and starts writing up the order. If the prospect provides the information, the order is written.

Note: The attitude implicit in the assumptive close, **positive expectancy,** must be present in all the other closes as well. **There is nothing more compelling than a positive, expectant attitude on the part of the salesperson.**

When using the assumptive close, be very sure of your ground.

"We'll schedule your installation for February 15th."

"What is your zip code, Mr. Case?"

"When should we arrange to have the packages picked up?"

"Which of your branches should we start with, Karen?"

If the prospect answers the above questions, he has bought—which meets the definition of a closing question.

2(a). Alternate Choice Close. This is a very popular and effective close because it gives the prospect a choice of two positive alternatives—either of which confirms the fact that he has bought.

"Is the Beta recorder satisfactory or would you prefer VHS?"

"Do I need a purchase order or can you just initial this agreement?"

"Would you prefer to purchase outright or is our lease plan more convenient?"

"Is Thursday at 10:00 a.m. or Friday at 11:00 a.m. better for you?"

*2(b). **Alternate Choice or Minor Point Close.*** Some people can't make a major decision so we present a "minor" or easy decision that, in effect, confirms the fact that the prospect has bought.

"Should we include a stand for the unit or do you have your own?"

"Do you prefer a hard or soft case for the camera?"

"Shall we install the deluxe floor mats or will you be taking the ones that come with the car?"

"Shall we send additional displays with the watches or do you have enough displays in stock?"

Once the prospect has answered the "minor" question, he has, in fact, acquiesced to a "major" purchase.

*3. **Impending Event/Need For Immediate Action Close.*** This is a good closing tactic to use when delay on the part of your prospect may cause him to miss an opportunity to gain a benefit or avoid a loss.

An example might be a change in interest rates, a new regulation going into effect shortly, price specials, limited availability of certain models, upcoming price increase, or the dollar getting weaker versus foreign currency.

Of course, it has to be legitimate to work.

"Mr. Prospect, if you leave Thanksgiving Day and return before noon on the following Saturday, you can fly at 70% of our regular fare. However, there is limited seating so I'll need to book your flight as soon as possible. If I can have your credit card number, we can get your tickets to you by Friday."

"We have only one of these models in stock. Shall I reserve it for you?"

4. Narrative or Favorable Reference Close. To induce your prospect to move that extra yard, you refer to a satisfied customer who faced a situation similar to the prospect's. It's used to eliminate his doubts and get him to take immediate action. Here's an ideal situation to use the "feel-felt-found" technique for overcoming objections:

> "Mr. Prospect, I can appreciate how you feel about changing carriers and retraining operators. Bill Daley, over at Superior Financial, felt the same way when we first talked. But he has found that his concerns were unwarranted. He had a smooth installation and the operators love our new system. You will experience the same excellent results. Let's get the ball rolling. When's the best time to start. How about the week of. . . ?"

5. Special Inducement Close. Similar to the impending event, the prospect is offered something "extra" for making his decision today. After summarizing the benefits, the salesperson says:

> "Mr. Prospect, you seem to like all these suits, and they look nice on you. You'll be happy to know that on these models, I can give you a $50.00 rebate on the second suit—and a $75.00 rebate on the third. This means a savings of $125.00. Because they're all a good fit, this is an excellent opportunity to buy all three and save money, don't you agree?"

6. Physical Action Close. In this tactic, you ask the prospect to physically do something such as check the features he likes or pick the locations in which to initiate the system. "Let's pick out a spot for the rack," is a way a book sales rep uses "physical action" to get his order for a new science fiction line.

You may take the physical action yourself, as when you say, "Let me call the warehouse to see if we can get you those models within ten days." Or, "Mr. Prospect, we'll set you up with a customer number and send you some preaddressed freight bills. Just fill in the consignee's name and address. When would you like your first pick up?"

7. "Why Not?" or Hidden Objection Close. When you have made several attempts at closing but have not moved the prospect, you need to uncover the reason the prospect is holding back—why he isn't buying.

You summarize the benefits as follows:

> "Mr. Prospect, if I understand you correctly, you'd like to increase the speed of your FAX operation without increasing your present costs. You've agreed that the full duplex capability, auto dialer, and document feeder will permit you to function with fewer machines and that our two-minute speed is far superior to your present equipment. You also agreed that we can do your job for less that you're presently spending and give you greater efficiency."

> "But Mr. Prospect, there seems to be something that's troubling you or that you have some doubts about. If you'll share it with me, I'll try my best to clarify it."

What you are trying to do is to uncover the real reason for the delay. Once you have done that, get the prospect to agree that if you can satisfy him on that point, he will move ahead.

*8. **Balance Sheet or Ben Franklin Close.*** There are many variations of this tactic, but essentially it involves a written summary of the pros and cons of doing the deal. Sometimes, seeing information in black and white helps the prospect make a decision.

Take a blank sheet of paper, draw a line down the middle, and title one side "reasons for" and the other side "reasons against."

Ask your prospect to list the reasons against first. Chances are he will mention initial investment and one or two other factors. When he's through, ask him if there is anything else he would like to include. Give him some time to think.

Now move to the reasons for. Ask him to list the reasons he would buy your product or service. Give him some help by providing reasons he has failed to come up with. By the end of this exercise, your list of reasons for should far outweigh the reasons against.

Conclude with "Mr. Prospect, I think you see in black and white that the reasons for making a decision to go ahead far outweigh the reasons against. Let's set a convenient time for getting started."

This kind of written comparison can also be effective in comparing your product or service with your competitor's. Write your company's name and your competitor's name at the top of a sheet of paper. On the left side of the paper, make a list of the product's most important features. Go through each feature and place check marks next to the features you offer and the ones your competitor offers. You should win this feature comparison.

9. Ask-for-the-Order Close. When you have exhausted all other possibilities, it may be necessary to confront the prospect and ask, "Mr. Prospect, may I have your go ahead for this program?"

This is a form of closed-end question and demands a yes or no answer. The preceding closes are less threatening and should be tried first. However, given a choice between asking and not asking for the order, always ask for the order no matter how you do it.

Some other ways your might phrase an ask-for-the-order close are:

"May I have your order?"
"What's our next step?"
"Can I add your name to our client list?"
"Sounds like you've got yourself a spanking new car?"
"Shall we call it a deal?"
"Should we move ahead?"

If after several attempts, your prospect still appears interested but balks at signing the order, try the following approaches:

"Bill, you seem to like what we have to offer—you apparently see the benefits—but something is holding you back."
"Bill, what does it take to get your business?"

Remain silent and wait for the response. Hopefully, you will either get a go ahead or learn the final or real obstacle to the close. Here is another close to use in this situation:

"Mr. Prospect, if you were me, selling you, what would you do now?"

The ball is in the prospect's court. Perhaps he will disclose what needs to be done to move ahead.

Rule 6 of Closing: The salesperson builds value into his offering by increasing its worth to the buyer through benefits.

What is "value?" Value is a measure of how strongly the buyer wants something—his personal evaluation of the worth of a product or service to him.

Value is not intrinsic to the product. By itself no product or service has value. Someone has to perceive value in the product. Value is a subjective judgment in the mind of the customer—his personal estimate of the benefits he will receive.

This is an exciting concept because it means that the salesperson can strongly influence the value of his offering to the customer. His success depends on his ability to relate the benefits to the buyer's wants and needs.

In a buying situation, the buyer is comparing what he will have to pay for the product with what he is going to get out of it.

If, in his mind, price outweighs value, there is no sale. If he sees price and value as being equal, there is a **possibility** of a sale. If the customer believes that the value exceeds the price, you've got an order!

How do you build value into your product or service? Here are some ways to build value:

- Know your product or service thoroughly.
- Know your prospect's business, applications, and customers.
- Understand your prospect's needs and the benefits he is looking for, intangible as well as tangible.
- Load the value side of the scale with benefits, benefits, benefits so that the price pales by comparison. Features justify a price. Benefits justify a purchase.
- Talk the language of value, emphasize how your offering will benefit the prospect more than any competitive product under consideration.

Talk quality, service, ease of operation, delivery, loaners, 800 numbers, trade-in value, financial arrangements, mechanical or technical service, personnel training, convenience, reputation, aesthetics, size, portability, consistency, ease of ordering—anything that proves the value of your product. Don't forget your own expertise and experience and the personal service you will render. They just may be the most important of all the value-added benefits you can offer.

Rule 7 of Closing: Amortize the price differential over the life of the product and compare it to the benefits your prospect will receive from the higher-price product.

No treatment of closing would be complete without addressing the universal objection: "Your price is too high. I can get it for less." When the objection is valid, not just a smoke screen, here is an effective way to handle the price objection.

A salesperson selling video monitors has made a demonstration and is confronted with the objection that the prospect can buy a competitive model for $400 less—a model that the prospect claims is "more or less" of equal quality to the proposed monitor.

After pointing out the benefits of his product again, the salesperson meets the same price objection. Finally, the salesperson says, "Mr. Prospect, if I could meet the price you've been quoted, would you give me the order?"

Note: This is a good qualifier. You will find out if price, indeed, is the real issue. Don't be surprised to find that it really isn't price, but simply a case of being out-sold. Price can be a convenient way for a prospect to let the losing salesperson off the hook without having to give the real reason for his choice.

If a prospect says no to your proposition, ask him why he would not choose your product if the price was equal. Try to uncover the real reason he is giving the order to your competitor. You may not be able to change his mind, but you may learn what you did wrong or failed to do right for the next time.

But let's return to our video salesperson and his question.

Salesperson: "Mr. Prospect, if I could meet the price you've been quoted, would you give me the order?"
Prospect (somewhat surprised): "Yes. If you can meet that price, you've got a deal."

Salesperson (pausing): "Why? Why, Mr. Prospect, if the price is the same, would you give me the order?"

Prospect: "Well, I think you have a little better quality product, and your company has a good reputation for service and you seem to know your business."

What the salesperson has done here is to get the prospect to verbalize the extra value he recognizes in the product. The next step, of course, is to convince him that the extra value he is getting is worth the additional price.

> Salesperson: "Let me see if I understand you, Mr. Prospect. You feel that our monitor has better picture quality, you acknowledge our good service, and you like the attention and ideas I've given you. Is that a fair statement?" Note: This is an example of using active listening and reflection.

> Prospect (grudgingly): "Ye-e-s, I suppose so."

> Salesperson: "Mr. Prospect, what do you estimate the useful life of this monitor to be?"

> Prospect: "About five years."

> Salesperson: "That's sixty months. If we divide the $400 difference by sixty months, that comes to $6.67 per month—is that right?"

> Prospect: "Well yes—I guess so."

> Salesperson: "Mr. Prospect, what this means is that for $6.67 a month or $1.50 a week, you'll be getting superior picture quality every time you use this monitor. In addition, you'll have trouble-free performance and the peace-of-mind that you'll get quick reliable service whenever you need it. And I'll be around to make sure your people know how to use the monitor. Isn't that worth only $6.67 a month?"

Let's review the technique used:

1. Determine the dollar difference between your offering and the lower-price competitive offering.
2. Ask the prospect if he would buy from you if you could match the price.
3. If he says yes, ask why. Get him to state the reasons in terms of product or service difference.

4. Restate those differences.
5. Ask the prospect the useful life of the product.
6. Convert into months or weeks and divide this into the differential amount to arrive at a monthly or weekly cost differential.
7. State the additional benefits he will receive for the small monthly difference.

Help the prospect to visualize how these additional benefits will accrue throughout the useful life of the product. He will in effect be paying for those missing benefits continuously by buying the lower-price brand. By paying a little more once, he will have the enjoyment of a quality product over and over again.

You may not close every deal with this technique, but you will get some you might not have closed. You will also ease the pain of those you lose by knowing that you gave it your best shot.

Rule 8 of Closing: Ask for an order on every sales call. An order is any action that moves the sale along.

Don't be shy about asking a prospect to buy something that you know he will benefit from. People squander their money on many useless things. You are doing them a favor when you convince them to make a decision that will enable them to gain a benefit or avoid a loss.

Prospects will never experience all the wonderful benefits of your offering until they become customers. Close positively and confidently. Don't be tentative about asking for the order. Customers expect it. If you don't ask, your competitor will. The worse thing that can happen to you is that the prospect says no.

Are you any worse off than before you asked? You didn't have the order then, either.

Let's review the eight rules of closing.

1. Regard closing as a natural step in the selling process.
2. Use trial closes, statements or questions that gain the prospect's acceptance throughout the entire selling process.
3. Watch your prospect like a hawk. Be alert for verbal and nonverbal buying signals and check them out with trial closes.

4. The decision to buy is first made in the mind of the salesperson. The prospect need only agree with that decision.
5. Learn several closing techniques that work in your business and have them ready at all times.
6. The salesperson builds value into his offering by increasing its worth to the buyer through benefits.
7. Amortize the price differential over the life of the product and compare it to the benefits your prospect will receive from the higher-price product.
8. Ask for an order on every sales call. An order is any action that moves the sale along.

The following poem illustrates the concept of building value into a product.

The Touch of the Master's Hand

'Twas battered and scarred, and the auctioneer
Thought it scarcely worth his while
To waste much time on the old violin
But he held it up with a smile:
"What am I bid, good folks," he cried
"Who'll start the bidding for me?"
"A dollar, a dollar," then, "Two!" "Only two?"
"Two dollars, and who'll make it three?"
"Three dollars, once; three dollars, twice;
Going for three" But, no,
From the room, far back, a gray-haired man
Came forward and picked up the bow;
Then, wiping the dust from the old violin,
And tightening the loose strings,
He played a melody pure and sweet,
As a caroling angel sings.
The music ceased, and the auctioneer,
With a voice that was quiet and low,
Said: "What am I bid for the old violin?"
And he held it up with the bow.
"A thousand dollars, and who'll make it two?"

"Two thousand, and who'll make it three?"
"Three thousand, once, three thousand, twice,
And going, and gone," said he.
The people cheered, but some of them cried,
"We do not quite understand.
What changed its worth?" Swift came the reply:
The Touch of a Master's Hand

—Author Unknown

Give your product or service the "touch" it needs to enhance its value to your prospects, and closing will become easier, more satisfying, and more profitable.

11
The Power of Goal Setting

Sometimes I feel like I'm drifting—as if my life has lost its purpose. I'm driving, pushing, working hard—but why?

I get so caught up in the process that I forget the reason for all the effort.

I need goals to keep me focused, to keep my life in balance, to remind myself of my values, to keep me on track.

It's so easy to wander off the mark.

Goals act as a magnet to pull me through the obstacles.

Where are you in your life? Do you know where you are headed? Are you satisfied with what you have achieved up to now? Suppose you could have the last five years to live over—would you do things differently? Would you have planned differently? Are you where you are today because you planned it that way?

Or have you just drifted into your present situation? Perhaps following someone else's plan for you—or maybe no plan at all.

There is nothing that will influence the success you achieve in sales more than the progress you make in the area of goal setting.

When you commit yourself to the realization of **specific, worthwhile, predetermined** goals, you join the ranks of the few who are true achievers.

The outstanding men and women who have made their marks on the selling profession are those with a strong sense of purpose, depth of commitment, and specific goals.

Paul Meyer, president of SMI International, makes this insightful observation concerning goals and success: "If you're not satisfied with the progress you're making, and feel capable of making, it's simply because your **goals** are not **clearly defined**."

The real significance of this statement is that most of us have achieved whatever we have wanted badly enough in life and were willing to pay the price for. We can continue to achieve if we decide what we really want and commit ourselves to making it happen.

Definite goals get definite results. Indefinite, vague, hazy goals may get no results.

Unfortunately, many of us don't know what we really want so we are reluctant to give a 100 percent effort to something that we are not really sure of. We need to make a commitment to something. There are no guarantees in life.

For the first five years I was in business, I was unconsciously preparing myself to fail. The way I was doing it was by continuously harboring doubts about whether I really wanted to be doing what I was doing. Once I made a total commitment, my career began to turn upward.

What are the benefits of written goals? Written goals **add a sense of value**. They make you take a look at yourself in terms of your expectations for yourself.

Written goals help you concentrate. When you have clear goals in mind you can see, hear, and feel more ways of reaching your goal that you ever dreamed possible. You develop a selective perception regarding your goals; that is, you begin to see your world in terms of your goals and are able to relate and connect seemingly unrelated ideas and events.

Written goals **add self-respect**. There is an intense satisfaction and self-confirmation in achieving something important to you. It's that psychological pat on the back that signifies "I set out to do it and I did it—and I can do it again," instead of "Gee, I was lucky to win that one, but how long will my luck hold out?"

Written goals provide **a sense of purpose and anticipation** to your life. It is exciting and fun to be moving toward accomplishments that are meaningful to you.

Written goals help in **decision making**. It is easier to decide on a course of action when you know what you are trying to achieve.

Written goals **save time**. When you have specific goals in mind, you are less likely to become distracted by irrelevant activities.

Written goals **reduce conflict and frustration**. By setting goals in all the areas of life that are important to you, (as you did in your Wheel of Life), you are less likely to end up frustrated and disappointed because you achieved goals in one area but left the remainder of your life in shambles.

Let's examine the key characteristics of a successful, personal goals program.

1. Your goals must be your own personal goals. This means that you take an objective, introspective look at what you really want out of life—not what mom, dad, or anyone else thinks you **should** want.

Your goals must be based on your needs, your values, your dreams. Consider your personality, talents, and abilities and your likes and dislikes. Decide what it is you want to be, to have, to do and make that the basis for your plan. Your goals must reflect what is uniquely important to you or you will not be motivated to give the very best that is in you to achieve your goals

2. Your goals must be comprehensive. Include all the areas of life that are important to you in your goals plan. This means taking into consideration the social, mental, religious/ethical, physical, financial, political, family, and career aspects of your life. They need not be given equal weight, and they may change from time to time, but you should evaluate them and arrive at a balance that reflects your own values and needs. It is important to work on the more intangible goal of "becoming" as well as the goal of acquiring.

3. Your goals must be realistic and attainable. To dig into your reservoir of untapped potential, you will need to challenge yourself. However, the goals you set should be doable with stretch and not be the "impossible dream." Of course, setting low goals will not result in the personal growth and development that a well-thought-out goals program can produce. On the other hand, unrealistically high goals will demotivate you and may result in a perpetual "guilt trip" because you are not achieving what you unrealistically set for yourself.

4. Your goals must be written and specific. Goals must be in writing or else they are easily forgotten. This is critical for a successful goals program. There are such tremendous demands on our time and intrusions into our awareness that it is imperative that we commit our goals to writing.

Writing will crystallize your thinking and crystallized thinking will motivate you into action. The palest ink lasts longer than the most enduring memory.

Your goals need to include target dates for completion as well as a way to be measured. You need to know whether you are winning or losing and that means making your goals specific and measurable. If you are going to lose weight, state how many pounds and by what date ("I'm going to lose fifteen pounds by February 10th") If you are setting earnings goals, what is the exact amount you want to achieve and by when? ("I will earn ten thousand dollars in commissions from new account sales in the next three months.") Target dates or deadlines add a timeliness and sense of urgency to the goal-setting process.

5. Your goals must include personality changes. What we are suggesting here is not to change your fundamental personality but to work on identifiable behaviors to become more effective professionally and personally.

For example, if you are not very good at making formal presentations to groups because you are reserved and lack confidence, you may need to work on your attitude as well as your technique.

If you tend to shoot from the hip and prefer spontaneity to planning but recognize that better preparation will result in better performance, then work on becoming better organized. Willingness to recognize the need for behavior change and to work toward personal improvement is one of the most important elements of goal setting.

6. You must make a firm commitment. Once you have decided what your goals are, "inked" them, set target dates, and made them measurable and specific, it's time to make the commitment to yourself to achieve your goals despite outside circumstances or regardless of what others may say, think, or do. Crystallize your thinking and close all the loopholes. Don't allow easy "outs" or excuses. Burn your bridges behind you. Steel your resolve and adopt an I-will-not-be-denied attitude. Take personal responsibility for your success.

Realistically, you can have virtually anything in life you want if you are willing to pay the price. People with ordinary talent and ability have accomplished extraordinary results because of a depth of commitment combined with persistence, enthusiasm, and planning (PEP).

7. *Visualize and think in terms of success.* See your goals as mentally accomplished. What will success appear like? How will you feel? What will you see, hear, taste, and smell? Put all your sensory acuity to work to create the picture of success in your mind's eye.

How does it feel to have that new title, office, home, or car? How has your relationship with friends, family, business associates, or the opposite sex changed? Get the picture in your mind's eye of how "smashing" you will look when you lose all that weight.

Close your mind to failure. Create the mental image of the person you will become when your goals are realized and put the "act as if" principle to work. "If you seek a virtue—act as if." Start acting like that person—right now!

You see, we don't plan to fail. We just fail to plan.

Your career, your family, your health, your life, are too important to leave to chance or to someone else's plan.

If you don't know where you're going, then any road will get you there. If you don't set goals for your life, you are a problem maker, not a problem solver.

Despite the fact that you will get little argument that goals are vital to achievement, most people don't set goals. Why?

Probably the most common reason that people don't set goals is because they are afraid they won't reach them. And if they can't reach them, aren't they "failures?" Suppose I set a goal to earn $75,000 this year and only earn $65,000? Haven't I failed?

Perhaps we don't know what failure is. The real failure is to set no goals and never challenge your potential. The real failure is not to try at all.

If you think you are beaten, you are!
If you think you dare not, you don't!
If you'd like to win, but think you can't,
It's almost a cinch that you won't.

If you think you'll lose, you're lost;
For out in the world we find
Success begins with a fellow's will;
It's all in the state of mind.

If you think you're outclassed, you are;
You've got to think high to rise.
You've got to be sure of yourself
Before you can win the prize.

Life's battles don't always go
To the strongest or fastest man;
But sooner or later the man who wins
Is the man who thinks he can!

—Author Unknown

Here are some other reasons for not setting goals:

Complacency — A why-rock-the-boat attitude. "Things are not as good as they could be, but I'm getting by, maybe not as well as some, but better than others."

Procrastination — "I'm not ready. It's not the right time. Someday, I'll get around to it."

Fate is in control syndrome — "I can't control my future. My boss, competition, the economy, outside influences—those are what counts. I'm just a little guy." Or, "What can I do? You just gotta be in the right place at the right time. Success is really a matter of luck." (Success really is a matter of luck. If you doubt it, just ask any failure.)

Don't know how — "Where do I start, how do you go about it, how do I know what I really want?"

Low self-concept — "I don't deserve to be successful. I'm just an ordinary person. There's nothing special about me."

It's too hard — "How can I look into the future, I'm having a tough time figuring out what's going to happen tomorrow. I'm thankful I can get through today. Let tomorrow take care of itself."

How To Set Up a Goals Program

There are three types of goals:
1. Long-range goals (six months to ten years)
2. Short-range goals (one week to six months)
3. Daily goals or activities (one day to one week)

A fourth type is not really a goal, it's a **dream**. However, dreams can become goals if we want them badly enough.

To get started on your goals program, get a three-ring binder, ruled paper, and four dividers for the four categories mentioned above.
1. Dream list
2. Long-range goals
3. Six-month goals
4. Daily to-do list

Title your binder "My Personal Plan of Action." If you don't have a binder handy right now, get some blank paper or use the forms provided on page ??? and let's start the process.

Step 1: *Develop a dream list.*

Most of us stopped dreaming when we realized that there was really no Santa Claus. We began to accept the reality that we would never experience many of the things we fantasized about as children.

Perhaps we have become reconciled to the reality that many of the good things in life are meant for others, that it's too late or too far out of our reach to realize our fondest desires.

This may be true for **some** of the things we dreamed about in the past. But unless we acknowledge our hopes and desires by writing them down, we are denying ourselves **any** chance of achieving them— even partially.

> It is a funny thing about life; if you refuse to accept anything but the best, you very often get it.
>
> —Somerset Maugham

Today, right now, you have permission to dream, to fantasize, to visualize, to conceptualize, to let your imagination run loose, to get your creative juices flowing.

Without giving mental recognition to whether you can achieve it or not, write down everything you have ever wanted to be, do, have, go, see, experience, taste, feel, hear, and smell. Let your pen take over and let your bottled up wishes, hopes, and desires flow onto the page. No restrictions, no limitations.

Put your dreams on paper. Nothing is too far out.

How was the trip? How did you feel writing those thoughts down? Did you visualize having accomplished some of those dreams? Did you limit yourself by what you believed you could achieve? Did you stay "within the dots"?

Work on your dream list for five minutes each day for the next week, adding more and more items to your list. Whenever anything pops into your mind, write it down. When you have a full list, review it, and put an "A" next to the six dreams you would most like to see come true in your lifetime. At this point, you will probably apply some practicality to your choices—the degree of possibility that they can be achieved.

After you have selected the six items from your dream list, choose the most important of the As and make that A1. The next most important item is A2 and so on until you have prioritized the six items.

Now create a separate page entitled "My Six Most Desired Dreams" and write them in declining order of importance. Next to each, put the date by which you would like to accomplish each dream. It is quite possible that the dates will be years away.

Step 2: Do a five- or ten-year projection.
Where do you want to be in five or ten years? What will your career be like? Your family situation? Your financial worth? Choose either five or ten years. If you are comfortable thinking ahead ten years, use the ten-year figure. In doing the next exercise, have your "My Six Most Desired Dreams" list handy and refer to it as you answer the questions.

You will probably experience some difficulty doing this exercise for the first time. You will feel that some of your responses are most like random thoughts rather than the way you really feel or think. There may not even be a clear pattern to your answers. That's OK. Just get your thoughts on paper so you can review them. Now complete "My Five- or Ten-Year Projection."

Dream List

_____

_____

_____

_____

_____

_____

_____

_____

_____

_____

_____

_____

_____

_____

_____

_____

_____

_____

_____

_____

_____

_____

_____

My Five- or Ten-Year Projection

(Answer these questions as if you were filling out this form five or ten years from right now.)

1. My age is _____

2. My occupation is (be as specific as possible) _____
    _____

3. My specific occupational responsibilities are _____
    _____
    _____

4.a. My specific annual income is $ _____

  b. The sources of my income are _____
    _____

5. My total net worth is $ _____

6. It is comprised of: Business interests $ _____ .
    Real estate $ _____   Commodities $ _____ .
    Securities $ _____   Sav./checking acct. $ _____ .
    Insurance $ _____   Retirement income $ _____ .
    Other $ _____ .

7. My nonbusiness responsibilities are _____
    _____
    _____

8. My hobbies or avocations are _____
    _____
    _____

9. My most important personal possessions are _____
    _____
    _____

10. Of my experiences in the last few years, the most pleasurable
    were _____
    _____
    _____
    _____

11. Of my experiences in the last few years, the ones that gave me
    the greatest sense of accomplishment were _____
    _____
    _____
    _____

12. In the last few years, several dramatic things have happened in
    my business and/or community that have interested me. Below
    is a summary of the highpoints, including a description of how
    I was involved in these events. _____
    _____
    _____
    _____

*   *   *   *   *

(Answer this from your present perspective.)
In reviewing my five- or ten-year projection, my most important
observations are: _____
_____
_____
_____

Now that you have completed the five- or ten-year projection, what
were your major observations? Was there any relationship to your dream
list?

Has any semblance of a long-range plan begun to form? Do you see your future as a continuation of your present path or will you make some sharp turns or changes? Is there anything you can do in the present to start moving toward your longer range goals?

Goal setting is not fantasizing, idle daydreaming, or a substitute for reality. It is not wishful thinking about the past or the future. It is not vague predictions of what might happen down the road.

Goal setting is building a bridge from the present to the future. It is turning thoughts into action, dreams into reality. It is deciding on what you want your future to be and then bringing the future into the present so you can do something about the future today. Years fly by so quickly, it is mind boggling.

You are bouncing a baby on your knee and in what seems to be a "wink" in time, the baby is a full-grown man or woman. You begin a job and suddenly you have been there fifteen years. Remember, it is only what you do in the present that will bring you closer to your long-range goals.

You have projected your future and perhaps have begun to formulate some long-range plans. To become motivated toward acting on these long-range goals, we must convert them into short-term goals that you can work on in the present.

Step 3: Develop a six-month goals program.
The next exercise, designed to help you establish your short-range goals, was inspired by noted sales trainer, Ron Willingham.

Take a blank sheet of 8½ in. x 11 in. paper and hold it so that the long sides are parallel to the floor and ceiling. Fold top to bottom first—then left to right. Now left to right again, making a small booklet. On the top right-hand corner of the booklet, write today's date. Entitle your booklet "Things I Want to Have Happen to Me in the Next Six Months," and put it aside temporarily.

Now review the following six-month goals list and on a blank sheet of paper, write the answer to any questions that are personally meaningful to you. Feel free to answer as many questions as you like.

Remember to answer the questions in the context of what you can achieve in the next six months. For example, if you would like to buy a new home, but six months is not a realistic time frame, write down some steps you can take in the next six months such as picking out the neighborhood, saving for a down payment, or arranging for financing.

Six-Month Goals

1. How much would you like to weigh?
2. How much money would you like to earn?
3. What specific habit would you like to develop?
4. What specific habit would you like to break?
5. What personality trait would you like to develop?
6. What kind of home would you like to own?
7. What improvement would you like to make in your present home?
8. What would you like to do on your next vacation?
9. How can you better communicate with your family members?
10. How can you better communicate with your coworkers?
11. What new office would you like to obtain?
12. What new position would you like to attain?
13. What new honor would you like to attain?
14. What specific person would you like to have as a closer friend?
15. What professional or occupational skill would you like to strengthen?
16. What new hobby would you like to begin?
17. What new activity would you like to begin?
18. What would eliminate pressures, stresses, or worries from your life?
19. What would solve a particular problem you have now?
20. What study habits would you like to acquire?
21. What specific improvements in your physical condition would you like to make?
22. What physical activity would you like to start?
23. How much money would you like to save each pay period?
24. What specific financial habit would you like to acquire?
25. What debts would you like to pay off?
26. What additional education would you like to have?
27. How much merchandise, goods, or services would you like to sell?
28. What would you like to do for your church or synagogue?
29. What would you like to do for your community?
30. What civic interest or public service would you like to be involved in?
31. What image would you like to communicate to others?
32. What would you have to do in order to influence others in a more desirable way?

33. What things can you do to build up members of your family?
34. What activities can you do with your family members
35. What common interests can you involve yourself in with other family members?
36. What spiritual goals would you like to set?
37. What spiritual qualities would you like to develop?
38. What other things would you like to have happen to you in the next six months?

After completing the list of goals, review your "Wheel of Life" (Chapter 2) and add any goals that your wheel suggests. Look at your dream list and write down anything that you can do in the next six months that will bring you closer to one of your six desired "dreams." You will want to also consider your five- or ten-year projection and add any short-range goals that come to mind. Feel free to add anything you want to accomplish in the next six months.

Go through the list and select your **six** most important goals, putting an A next to each one. After you have done this, review each of the six goals and ask yourself this question, "Will I make an impact on my life, push out my Wheel of Life, if I achieve this goal? If your answer is yes, ask yourself another question, "Am I willing to pay the price in terms of **time, money, effort, and risk?**"

If you can answer yes to the above, you have got yourself a goal. If you are hesitating or doubtful, forget it. It's really not a goal, it's a wish.

Unfortunately, we are not motivated by wishes—only goals.

Once you have selected six goals that you are committed to work toward (less is OK if that's all that qualify), prioritize them in order of importance by making your most important goal A1, next most important, A2, and so forth.

Which areas of your life are affected by these goals? Ideally, several areas will be affected. Some goals will strengthen more than one spoke of the wheel. Doing physical exercise with the family relates to both the physical and family areas. Joining a neighborhood book club might impact your social and mental areas.

I suggest you write your six month goals in two places: in your Personal Plan of Action binder and in the little paper booklet you have constructed.

Write one goal on each page of your paper booklet. Write the goals as if they are already happening, in the present tense, so that you can visualize what it will be like when you achieve the goals.

For example, if one of your goals is to lose twenty pounds in a six-month period and you now weigh one hundred thirty-eight, you might write your goal as follows:
"I weigh one hundred eighteen pounds, and I look and feel terrific!"

Notice that the goal is written in the first person singular, ("I" or "me"), uses the present tense, and includes the WIIFM (what's in it for me) or benefit.

Write each goal on a separate page of your goals booklet. This is important: place your six-month goals booklet in your pocket diary so you have it with you at all times. When you make out your daily to-do list each day, review your six-month goals booklet to see what activities you can do to move you closer to one of your six-month goals.

Congratulations, you have now joined the top 3 percent of the population with written and specific goals and with a deadline for achievement.

Step 4: *Writing a plan of action.*
Now that you have your goals, how do you begin to work on them? You need to devise a plan of action for each of your goals.

You may want to start with only one of your six-month goals— perhaps the A1. It is not necessary to work on all your goals at one time.

The following form (Figure 11-1) gives you an easy-to-follow format for developing an action plan.

1. At the top of the Goals Plan of Action form, write your goal as clearly and as specifically as you can. Also write the planned completion date.

2. Next, in the box titled Obstacles and Roadblocks, list all the things that could possibly prevent you from achieving your goal. Let it all out. Include internal as well as external factors such as procrastination, fear of failure, and limited time available.

Figure 11-1
Goals Plan of Action

GOAL: _____
_____
_____
_____

OBSTACLES AND ROADBLOCKS: _____
_____
_____
_____
_____

SOLUTIONS: (List the specific steps you will   TARGET
take to accomplish the goal and   DATES:
overcome obstacles.)

_____
_____
_____
_____
_____
_____
_____
_____

REWARDS AND BENEFITS: _____
_____
_____
_____

METHOD OF KEEPING SCORE:

DATE   PROGRESS TO DATE

3. In the Solutions box, list each obstacle and the steps you will take to overcome it. Next to each solution, put a target date, the date you will complete that step. This is the place to list all the things you will need to do in order to reach your goal. These become subgoals. By breaking the overall goal into smaller goals, the major goal does not appear to be as difficult or overwhelming as you first thought.

4. In Rewards and Benefits, write what you will get out of accomplishing your goal, the WIIFM. This is very important because we are motivated by end-result benefits, not the process. Write how it will sound, look, feel, taste, and smell when your goal is realized.

5. Method of Keeping Score. For a very short-range goal, say a week or two, it may not be necessary to establish check points or bench marks. But for a long-range goal, it is a good idea to measure your progress to date. Circumstances may dictate that you alter your action plan, increase the effort, or even change the goal. Set up the dates when you will review your progress. If others are involved in your goal, you may want to set up a meeting schedule or get periodic reports on their progress to date.

Write an action plan for each of your six-month goals and place it in the six-months goals section of your Personal Plan of Action binder.

Plan to spend time on your Personal Plan of Action binder each week. Update your dream list, review your five- or ten-year projection, check your six-month goals, and your plan of action for each goal. Life is a constant process of change and adjustment.

The chapter on time organization shows you how to connect your long-range goals to your daily activities.

If you don't have clearly defined personal goals, you will go through life in a reactive mode, responding to things that happen to you, instead of making things happen for you. Without goals, we often find ourselves engulfed in a flood of activity, very much like running a place. Many people rationalize their predicament by blaming it on the demands of their job, their boss, their customers, family, friends, and any circumstances beyond their control. How can you be expected to be concerned about the future when you are so busy contending with the present?

Goals will enable you to stay in charge of your time—and your life.

Summary

1. Goal setting begins with introspection and decisions as to what you want out of your life.

2. A person is rarely 100 percent sure that his goals are what he really wants or are "forever," but you need to make a commitment to something that you can give a 100 percent effort to.

3. Do a long-term projection to learn where you would like to be in the future. Determine if your present direction is getting you there. If not, consider change.

4. Set short-term goals (six months or less) to provide motivation and the satisfaction of achievement.

5. Make a daily-to-do list setting priorities on your activities. Include tasks that are aimed at long-range goals (chapter twelve).

6. Start with As not Cs (chapter 12).

7. It is not the number of goals you have, but the fact that you are working on quality goals with purpose and commitment that counts.

To be sure, each of us answers to someone or something outside of ourselves, and to some extent, external factors do control our activities. However, without a written Personal Plan of Action that addresses all of the areas of life that are important to you it is easy to fall into the trap of marching to someone else's drumbeat. Don't allow this to happen. Take control of your life through the power of goal setting.

12
Making Your Time Pay Off

*It's a constant internal battle for me to be preactive—
that is—to initiate my own activities and projects. I'm
always thinking and scheming about where my next
piece of business will come from. My wife calls it
worrying. Is that what it is?*

*Sometimes I think it would be great to have a job where
someone else plans my schedule and all I have to do is
follow it.*

*There are times when I know what tasks I **ought** to be
doing but end up doing what I want to do or **like** to do. I
rationalize to myself that they are equally important. This self-
deception shows up in my sales figures.*
  *It's great to have long-range goals, but when do you have
the time to work on them when you're fighting fires all the
time? I can't even get half the things done I need to do—let
alone long-range stuff.*

Is there a magic formula to good time management?

I think not. We all have the ability to make excellent use of our
time. After all, being organized has nothing to do with genetics, body
chemistry, or what neighborhood you grew up in. It is simply a matter
of habit—the habit of thinking ahead and planning.

The phrase "time management" is really a misnomer. We can't really
manage time. Time is inexorably passing even as you read this book.
You can't stop it, speed it up, or postpone it. Each of us has access
to all the time there is, every 60-minute hour, 24-hour day, and 168-
hour week.

What we can manage is ourselves and how we use our time so that we get the most out of it.

Salespeople Have Different Time Problems

Salespeople, unlike factory workers or administrative personnel, are on their own much of the time and need to generate their own activity. This demands strong, disciplined work habits.

Most salespeople are conscientious about their jobs and want to produce "a good day's work for a good day's pay." We are not always entertaining customers or on the golf course as our critics would have you think. (Even when we are, it's for a purpose and not just fun and games).

But putting in a "good day's work" can take different forms. Salespeople, in their need to justify to themselves that they are "working" may spend an inordinate amount of time on tasks such as:
• Making repetitive call backs on existing customers.
• Organizing records and manuals.
• Preparing elegant proposals to "iffy" prospects.
• Overservicing existing accounts.
• Procrastinating over complaints and problems.
• Meticulously filling out call reports, expense reports, and other forms during prime selling hours.
• Attending meetings, training programs, and seminars.
• Reading books and articles on selling or business.

Although these activities are worthwhile, you have to honestly ask yourself if you are doing them as a substitute for the riskier, less comfortable tasks such as:
• Prospecting for new business.
• Making selling presentations to qualified prospects and buyers.
• Closing (asking for the order).

It is not only how **much** time you spend on your job but **where** you spend it that counts. And the way you spend your time can be influenced by your personality style.

If you are nonconfrontive and service minded, you may rationalize that you should be developing relationships with existing clients (who you are comfortable with) instead of dealing with your call reluctance (the fear of risking rejection) by contacting people who don't know you or your company.

The way to avoid getting trapped into low payoff activities is to set realistic but challenging productivity goals for yourself. Examples are goals for number of phone dials, contacts, appointments, demonstrations, and new accounts. Even setting goals to call on presidents and vice presidents instead of purchasing agents or office managers is a good use of time. You might set a goal to call on one top executive each week, gradually building your confidence. Spending your selling time with buyers who have the authority to say yes will definitely up your return on time invested.

If management doesn't set productivity or "input" goals for you (or if you are self-employed) take the initiative to set them for yourself. Do some honest introspection and identify the selling skills where you need improvement as well as the behaviors that are your lesser strengths. Consciously work on these, breaking out of your comfort zone.

"You must always do what you're afraid to do," advises Penn State football coach, Joe Paterno. "Winners take risks."

As professional salespeople, our three most important activities in order of importance are:

1. Getting face to face with qualified prospects in order to sell
2. Scheduling appointments with qualified prospects
3. Gathering information on qualified prospects to complete step two and then step one.

All the other activities support these three.

Let's not lose sight of what selling is all about—getting business.

Where should you be spending your time? If you hired yourself as a consultant to improve your productivity, what advice would you give yourself?

What types of prospects and customers would you suggest that you concentrate on? How should you allocate your time? How much of your time should you spend on prospecting for new business? 90 percent, 60 percent, 30 percent, or 10 percent? How about cultivating existing accounts, 50 percent, 25 percent, 10 percent? Handling requests for information and servicing customers, 30 percent, 20 percent, 10 percent, 5 percent? How about educational activities such as product knowledge, applications, and selling skills, 15 percent, 5 percent, 2 percent?

Good time management begins with determining where and how you should be spending your time and assigning priorities. If your territory is new and you do not have many existing customers, most of your time will be spent in prospecting. If you have a well-developed client base that produces considerable repeat business, you will devote most of your time to existing accounts, maintaining relationships and penetrating into other areas.

Of course, once you have set your priorities you must put the plan into action. Anything you hope to acquire or accomplish will only happen as a result of the action you put into your desires, ambitions, and habits.

The Pareto Principle

Pareto was an Italian mathematician who originated the famous 80/20 rule mentioned earlier. What he discovered was that only 20 percent of the total effort usually produces 80 percent of the results. For example, 20 percent of a salesforce accounts for 80 percent of the revenues, 80 percent of sales is done in 20 percent of the product line, 20 percent of the prospects produce 80 percent of the business.

The message is to identify and concentrate your time and effort on the 20 percent of your activities that produce 80 percent of your accomplishments.

How are you managing your time now?

Here are twenty-nine tips on how to get a bigger payoff on the selling time you invest.

1. Start early—get a jump on the day, traffic, and competition. (Much of this book was written between 6:00 A.M. and 9:00 A.M.)

2. Have a plan for every day with your activities prioritized. Concentrate on the two or three most important goals for the day.

3. "Do your paperwork when it's dark, early in the morning or after 5:00 P.M. Save the prime-time selling hours for SELLING." This advice comes from the president of a successful professional video dealership.

4. Double check before each call to make sure you have your sales kit in order.

5. Call by appointment—all professionals do.

6. Confirm appointments in advance.

7. Use travel and waiting time. Listen to cassettes on motivation or selling skills while driving. Bring reading material for when you are kept waiting.

8. Organize your phone calls in order of importance or urgency. Know your objective and the subjects you want to cover.

9. Learn the best hours to contact customers and prospects. It might be before 8:00 A.M. or after 7:00 P.M.

10. Schedule your driving time and routes when and where traffic is lightest.

11. Carry extra prospect cards and have an alternate plan in case your appointment is canceled unexpectedly.

12. Carry loose change for tolls and phone calls.

13. Use breakfast meetings as a good time to see prospects and customers.

14. Use lunch hours (noon to 2:00 P.M.) for entertaining prospects and customers, travel time, reports, and phone calls.

15. Keep an accurate record of how you spend your time for one week in fifteen minute segments. Then analyze it to see where you can save time.

16. Limit the time you spend waiting to see a prospect.

17. Include prospecting time in each daily plan to develop new business.

18. Carry a dictating unit or notebook to jot down pertinent notes and comments while fresh in your mind.

19. Do important tasks when you are at the "top of your game."

20. Do some physical exercise to keep fit and mentally tuned. Purposely park your car one quarter mile from a prospect's office and walk briskly. Do this just twice a day and you will walk a mile without realizing it.

21. Handle paper work only once.

22. Schedule calls at "off hours" or even weekends if that is the best time to see an important prospect.

23. Be selective in your business reading. Read newspapers, books, and magazines that give you the background information you need to support your selling efforts. In addition to your own industry publications, these might include *Business Week*, the *New York Times*, and the *Wall Street Journal*.

24. Develop the habit of making minor decisions quickly. If the "downside" risk is small, don't agonize, do it!

25. Set aside a certain period of each day for recordkeeping and planning. The evening is an ideal time.

26. Work on your presentation so you can bend it to your prospect's time constraints.

27. "Smell the roses." Have some fun each day. Keep life in perspective. A sense of humor is a great selling asset. Laughter is food for the soul.

28. Take advantage of existing technology to make your job easier. Car phones save time and reduce stress. Computers and data-communications equipment can take your messages or distribute them, write your letters, store data, and enable you to communicate more effectively.

29. Use pre-call planning to make each sales call more effective.

Daily Time Planning
(Bringing the Future into the Present)

Most people prepare a daily to-do list. Some use their pocket planner or diaries. Others use a printed form or even a plain piece of paper. The form isn't important, what **is** important is that you prioritize your daily activities. What is also **important** is to include activities that bring you closer to your **long-range** goals.

Figure 12-1 shows an example of a daily time planner designed to enable you to do a better job of planning your day. The best time for planning your next day's activities is at the conclusion of the present one.

Here is how to use the form. In the left-hand column headed Things to Do Tomorrow, write down everything and anything you would like to accomplish tomorrow. Don't worry about the order of importance or even if you will have the time to do them. Just get everything you can think of on paper. Remember to include some fun things. We need to program fun into our lives.

Each day, when you prepare your daily to do list, lay your six-month goals booklet along side (chapter eleven). Add at least one or two activities to your daily to do that will bring you closer to one of your six-month goals.

This step is important because it is only what you do in the present that will get you closer to a long-range goal.

Figure 12-1
DAILY TIME PLANNER

Date: /   /

THINGS TO DO TOMORROW	A	IMPERATIVE	
_____		1 _____	
_____		2 _____	
_____		3 _____	
_____		4 _____	
_____		5 _____	
_____		6 _____	
_____		7 _____	
_____		8 _____	
_____		9 _____	
_____		IMPORTANT	
_____		1 _____	
_____		2 _____	
_____		3 _____	
_____		4 _____	
_____		5 _____	
_____		6 _____	
_____		7 _____	
_____		8 _____	
_____		9 _____	

GOOD THINGS THAT HAPPENED TODAY
_____
_____
_____
_____
_____
_____

A — Items checked are daily short-term goals that build toward my specific
longer-term goals

After your list is complete, you are ready to start setting priorities using the "ABC" method. Select the **three** most important tasks you have got to do tomorrow and write an A in the left margin next to each. Choose the next three or four most important items and make them Bs. The rest are Cs. Now select your most important A and make that your A1. The next most important A is A2 and so forth. Do the same for your Bs and Cs.

Now review your list and put a check mark to the right of each activity that is bringing you closer to a six-month goal. If you go too many days without a check mark in the right-hand column, what does it mean?

It means that you are not building toward longer-range goals. Remember, it is only what you do in the present that will get you to a longer range goal.

You have now prioritized each of your activities. We are ready to move the A items to the Imperative box, and the Bs and Cs to the Important box of your daily time planner (Figure 12-1). Place the imperative A items in order of importance or chronologically, whichever makes more sense to you. Bs go into the Important box followed by Cs. As you transfer an activity from the Things to Do Tomorrow column, cross it out.

Your daily time planner is now complete. You are ready to take action.

By setting priorities and by including activities that relate to your longer-range goals, you are in command of your time and your life. You no longer simply respond to events, you are starting to shape them. You're not just reacting, you're preacting. You're not retaliating, you're instigating.

The next important principle is to start with As not Cs. Don't be tempted to do the easy Bs and Cs at the expense of your As.

Spending time on an A, even for ten minutes, may be many times more productive than knocking off low-value Cs.

Of course, you may get a call from your boss or a key customer that will turn into your overwhelming A1 and back up all your other As, but you still have a plan, and you'll get back on track.

The key to good time organization is not necessarily doing things right but rather doing the **right** things.

A beautiful job of rearranging your files may not be nearly as productive as a telephone prospecting session that nets even one good appointment.

Of course, optimal use of your time is doing the **right** things **right!** Prioritize your activities each day and make sure you are working toward longer-range goals. Measure your daily accomplishments by how many genuine A activities you have completed.

When you begin your next day's daily to-do list, transfer all the activities that you did not complete to the Things to Do Tomorrow column and begin the process again.

As you move through the day, ask yourself the question, "What is the most important task I should be working on right now? Once you have answered that question, adopt a do-it-now attitude.

Make sure the activities that you've designated A are truly A activities.

Some of them will be things you don't look forward to doing—like informing a customer that his delivery will be delayed; calling to collect a long-past-due account; or pacifying an angry, dissatisfied user.

If they are A tasks or high Bs, do them first, get them out of the way. You will feel better the rest of the day and be less pressured and more able to focus on the positives.

Now that we have looked at ways to use your time more productively, let's examine some things that salespeople do to waste time.

How Salespeople Waste Time

Salespeople waste a lot of valuable time by:

1. Spending excessive time in the office

Unless you are getting appointments or having prospective clients visit you, you need to be where the action is—in the field.

2. Not qualifying prospects

You have a limited amount of time as well as emotional energy. Don't waste it on "deadbeats" and information seekers. Make sure you are talking to a decision maker who has a need and money and who wants to have the need satisfied.

3. Being reluctant to ask for the order

If you don't ask, you will make unnecessary call-backs and lose sales.

4. Starting late/finishing early

A surefire formula for failure. There just is no substitute for hard work.

5. Not calling for appointments

Results in "no-shows" and lost time. Also unprofessional.

6. Not planning their territories

Leads to unnecessary travel time and less time in front of prospects.

7. Not keeping good records

Salesperson covers same ground, misses important points, and lacks continuity with account.

8. Making calls on non-decision-makers

Results in stalls, put-offs, and no decisions.

9. Making unplanned sales calls

Salesperson appears rambling, unprofessional, and wastes prospect's time (usually only once).

10. Having a lack of clear goals

Purpose and commitment are lacking. Salesperson works on low-priority items. Temporary setbacks are blown out of proportion and cause demotivation and slackened effort.

11. Making too many calls on the same account

Is evidence of a lack of enough prospects, a failure to recognize non-buyers, or a reluctance to ask for the order.

12. Worrying and being negative

Salesperson wastes time and energy dwelling on un-favorable business condi-tions, competition, and product features that are lacking. Negative thoughts become self-fulfilling prophecies.

13. Not using driving and waiting time effectively

This time could be spent on cassette learning, read-ing, or paperwork.

14. Not working on high-priority tasks

Get momentary satisfac-tion from doing "C" tasks while the main job is left undone.

Summary

1. Effective time management begins with goals: long- and short-range. Spend, no invest, your time in those activities that have the biggest payoff for you.

2. Goal setting begins with introspection and decisions as to what you want out of **your** life.

3. A person is rarely 100-percent sure that his goals are what he **really** wants or are "forever," but you need to make a commitment to something that you can give a 100 percent effort.

4. Make a long-term projection to learn where you would like to be in the future. Determine if your present direction is getting you there. If not, consider change.

5. Set short-term goals, six months or less, to provide motivation and the satisfaction of achievement.

6. Make a daily to-do list setting **priorities** on your activities. Include tasks that are aimed at longer-range goals.

7. Start with As not Cs.

8. Remember to smell the roses—have some fun!

9. It is not the number of goals you have, but the fact that you are working on quality goals with purpose and commitment that counts.

10. With persistence, enthusiasm, and planning (the PEP formula) anything is possible.

13
Breaking Slumps

It seems that at times, everything dries up. The phone stops ringing, the mail is all about things to buy, and there are no leads or inquiries. I wonder if it's ever going to change—these peaks and valleys—the great depressions?

Where is all that enthusiasm and confidence I had? It seems to have disappeared. A few weeks ago I couldn't get out of the way of an order. But now . . .?

What am I doing wrong? Am I pressing too hard or not hard enough? I could sure use an easy one now.

Did you ever get the feeling you've plateaued—leveled off? How about "burned out," demotivated? You know something's wrong, but you can't put your finger on it.

Wouldn't it be nice to have some kind of troubleshooting guide like the one in the back of your VCR or microwave operation manual? You know the kind that has:

Symptom: No power.
           Power indicator does not light.
Possible Cause: AC line cord is disconnected.
           Electrical outlet defective.
Suggested Solution: Plug in AC line cord.
           Check outlet and fuse or circuit breaker.

Well, that's what this chapter is all about. It's a troubleshooting guide for salespeople.

This chapter presents the symptoms of, probable causes of, and suggested solutions to your selling problems. Chances are that you will experience some of these symptoms during your sales career.

Symptom 1: Not enough activity. Your inquiries are down. Your leads are drying up. You have too few A prospects.

Probable Causes:
- Not enough prospecting for new business
- Too much time servicing or calling back on accounts that are not ready to buy
- Prospecting techniques need polishing
- Not asking for enough referrals
- Not persistent in breaking through invalid objections and getting the appointment
- Too comfortable calling on accounts where you are accepted but the potential is not really there
- Not enough mailings, advertising, and promotion

Suggested Solutions:
1. Start spending more time on prospecting.
2. Set specific prospecting goals for:
   - Mailings (send five letters each day; three days later, make a follow-up call on each letter)
   - Dials
   - Contacts
   - Appointments
   - Referrals (Get remotivated by calling on customers presently benefiting from your product or service; get three referrals from each of those customers)
3. Fine tune your telephone scripts.
4. Work on objection-handling methods.
5. Try new or different prospecting sources: new lists, associations, networking organizations, new directories, former customers, low-volume accounts who may have grown; set up seminars; give talks, be in contact with people.
6. Tape your calls and play them back. See what you can correct and where you can improve.
7. Read books, listen to cassettes, and attend courses on prospecting. Review chapters three and four of this book.

Symptom 2: Poor closing average.

Probable Causes:
- Not enough prospects
- Not establishing trust and rapport with prospects
- Not qualifying prospects properly (review chapter seven)
  — Not identifying the decision maker(s)
  — Not uncovering the definite needs
  — Failing to determine ability to pay
  — Not creating a sense of immediacy and urgency
- Trying to close before all other steps in sales process are covered
- Poor closing techniques (review chapter ten)
- Not selling **benefits** and **value**
- Fear of price objection that is subliminally transmitted to your prospects
- Lack of confidence and enthusiasm in your product or service
- Not asking for the order enough times
- Permitting prospects to sell you on why they don't need what you are selling
- Low self-concept (you don't really believe you deserve the business)
- Asking for a bigger bite than your prospects can digest
- Making unrealistic claims about your product or service
- Not convincing prospects that they will realize the benefits you have promised

Suggested Solutions:
1. Have a lot of prospects; selling is a numbers game. Make the law of averages work for you.
2. Have a lot of prospects; losing one sale will not seem so traumatic.
3. Have a lot of prospects; it will raise your self-confidence level.
4. Build trust. Keep the prospect's WIIFM in mind at all times. Don't get too anxious.
5. Prioritize closable prospects. Work on the ones that are most closable.
6. Qualify **early** in the selling cycle so you are not wasting a lot of time on prospects who cannot buy.
7. Get agreement and take the buyer's temperature through trial closes.
8. Forget about your commission and quota. Sell benefits, benefits, benefits.

9. Make it easy for your prospects to buy. Offer them a money-back guarantee, free trials, or extended terms. Sell a small order as a test.
10. Use testimonials, client visits, demonstrations, and independent reports as proof to back up your claims.

Symptom 3: You're demotivated, depressed, burned out. You don't seem to enjoy what you're doing anymore.

Probable Causes:
- Working too hard (not enough play)
- Business down (not making quota)
- Lost big deal or large account
- Personal problems outside of business
- Feel quota is unrealistic
- Believe commission plan is inequitable
- Poor communication with superiors
- A lack of personal goals
- Not enough prospects (insufficient activity)
- Overexposed to negative influences of individuals who themselves are demotivated and dissatisfied and who blame others for their failure

Suggested Solutions:
1. Be honest with yourself. What is the real problem? Is it outside factors such as competition and business conditions or are your own negative attitudes the cause of the problem? Everyone experiences rejection and disappointment. It is how you react that determines where you go from there. One deal or one account more or less will not make the difference in a successful career. You are probably a lot closer to success than you think. Persistence is the key. Life is **not** an undefeated season.
2. Set realistic goals for yourself. Put them in writing (review chapter eleven). Let your goals motivate you into action. They will act as a magnet to pull you through. Let yourself win. Even getting an appointment is a win. Reward yourself when you do. Have some fun.
3. If your problem is personal and requires professional help, get it! Don't procrastinate. Everyone needs help at some time or other.

There is no stigma in recognizing a problem and seeking a resolution. That's being **smart**.

4. If you feel your quota is unrealistic, discuss it with your manager. Keep an open mind to his viewpoint. Have evidence to back up your claims. Anticipate his arguments. Treat this meeting as a sales call. Plan it out and have an objective.

5. Inactivity is a demotivater. You have too much time to dwell on the negatives. A salesperson's mission is to sell and this means getting face to face with prospects. Do anything to stimulate activity. Get on the phone and ask for appointments, request referrals, have lunch with one or two key customers each week, get testimonial letters. Do something, anything constructive.

6. Work on your attitude. Listen to motivational tapes, read motivational books.

7. Spend time with "winners," those individuals who are successful. Get exposed to their attitudes, habits, and techniques. Make sales calls with them, pick their brains. It is worth buying a beer or even a dinner to get ideas from someone who is making it happen. Distance yourself from the gloom-and-doomers who blame everyone but themselves for their lack of success.

8. Be long-range oriented. Use your intuitor style. Look at the big picture. Start doing the things that you know are right with the positive expectancy that you will get the results down the line. It may take a little longer than you expected. Most things do, but it will happen. "If you keep doing the right things, you'll get the right results." This is a philosophy I've lived by for my entire career.

9. If you are physically and mentally tired because of a very concentrated effort over a period of time, reward yourself with a vacation, even if it's just a few days. Get away from the business and focus your energies on something else such as a hobby, family, relaxation, anything. You will come back with renewed vigor and a happier outlook.

10. Visit a few satisfied users and get "resold" on your own product by finding out how they are benefiting from what you sold them. You may get some ideas for selling new business that you haven't considered.

11. Get plenty of exercise. Exercise sharpens the mental faculties as well as tuning you up physically.

12. If after honest reflection and introspection you come to the objective conclusion that the product, the territory, and company policies or politics are preventing you from realizing your true potential, and nothing can be remedied, then you should seriously consider making a change.

13. Review the first two chapters of this book.

Symptom 4: Not enough time. You're harried, pressured, rushed. You're feeling guilty.

Possible Cause:
- Not taking time each day to think and plan
- Not putting a dollar value on your time and activities and working on those high dollar activities first
- Letting old, ineffective habits dictate what you do and how you do it
- Not working enough hours
- Working too many hours
- Being a perfectionist
- Not delegating
- Having unrealistic goals
- Procrastinating
- Taking on too much, too quickly
- Not saying no where necessary and appropriate
- Reacting to events and the needs of others instead of deciding on priorities
- Not planning
- Confusing activity with productivity and becoming engulfed in activity
- Taking on responsibilities that rightfully belong to others
- Placing unrealistic expectations on yourself (or others) and feeling disappointed and guilty when those expectations are not met
- Substituting others' value systems for your own
- Not giving yourself sufficient credit for your accomplishments and properly savoring your victories

Suggested Solutions:
1. Have a clear set of prioritized goals and work on the activities necessary to achieve those goals.

2. Make a daily to-do list and work on the A tasks first.
3. Keep score on your progress.
4. Plan your work, then work your plan.
5. Adopt a do-it-now philosophy. Begin work on all A goals immediately, even if it's just for a little while. Once you start, chances are you will continue to pursue that goal.
6. Work when you are at your best. If you are a morning person, do your most demanding tasks in the morning.
7. Eliminate anything in your routine that is time consuming and that doesn't have a big payoff. We tend to do what we like to do and can easily rationalize that it is also important. Perhaps a one-hour coffee break with the gang can be cut down to fifteen minutes with the balance devoted to an A priority. Analyze your routines and habits and see where you can save wasted time.
8. Keep a record of your time for one week in fifteen minute segments, then analyze it carefully. It is surprising what you will learn. Most of our time is wasted in small bites.
9. Make and confirm appointments on the phone.
10. Cut down on travel time. Group appointments geographically.
11. Make sure you work on activities that are rightfully yours and not others. Don't become a "rescuer" by taking on other people's responsibilities. You not only deprive others of the challenge of facing their own problems when you become a rescuer, but eventually rescuers become preceived as "persecuters" and ultimately become "victims" themselves.
12. Review the chapters on goal setting and time management.
13. Don't give up. If you keep doing the right thing, you will eventually get the right results.

So there you have it, your troubleshooting guide for breaking slumps and getting back in winning form.

You have it within you to be a successful salesperson. It's not the company, product, market, or competition that will determine how successful you will be. Neither is it luck or chance.

Your success will be a result of your own attitudes and actions. If you believe you can make it and back that belief up with effort, nothing can stand in your way.

Every one of us was born to win, and we were equipped with all the mechanisms necessary to do it.

You've got a powerful eight-cylinder engine that is your mind and body. If you're only using two or three of these cylinders, you're just making your ride to the top slower and tougher for yourself.

You owe it to yourself to be the best you can be. Persistence, enthusiasm, and planning, the PEP formula, will help you realize your full potential as a sales professional.

In this book, I have shared the skills and attitudes that have helped me enjoy a rewarding career as a professional salesperson. They can do the same for you.

Put them into action, today!

Good luck.

> "Whatever you vividly imagine
> Ardently desire
> Sincerely believe
> and
> Enthusiastically act upon
> Must inevitably come to pass."
> —Paul Meyer
> President
> Success Motivation International